For Amit, Papa and Ma

For all those times when
only a cake will do

My Little Cake Tin

Over 70 Versatile, Beautiful,
Flavourful Bakes Using Just One Tin

Tarunima Sinha

Photography by Kim Lightbody

Hardie Grant

QUADRILLE

Introduction

Sometimes I think about my journey – did it all start with this humble chapati tin, which was repurposed as a cake tin in my parents' kitchen in India? Was this tin always meant to be a big part of my life?

I did not plan to become a baker. I studied textiles and design, and had a short career working as a bridalwear designer. However, I always enjoyed baking and cooking for people – I found myself experimenting with food at any given opportunity.

I grew up in a sleepy little town in northeast India, which had only a couple of bakeries back then. The simplest of cakes – Victoria sponge, carrot cake, lemon drizzle – were alien to me. My first taste of cake came from a small bakery shop that sold marble cake and pineapple cream cake. Papa would treat us to whatever we wanted there. He would also always buy two savoury onion breads – we would share one in the car on the way home.

At the age of 10, I baked my first cake – a simple marble cake – in my grandmother's 70-year-old aluminium chapati tin. My family home had a small, round, temperamental countertop oven. It only worked if the plug was positioned a certain way. Between the dodgy plug and the random power cuts we would have, baking was an act of complete faith. But, over the years, that oven baked many more marble cakes.

Fast-forward to 2001, when my life in the UK began: baking took on a whole new meaning. I had a proper oven for the very first time, access to all the cakes that London had to offer and a plethora of baking books to read. I began baking for friends, neighbours, family – anyone willing to eat cake! Cake became a medium through which to share joy – both for special occasions and just for something to share over a cup of tea.

Little did I know then that baking would become more than just a hobby. It was to become a purpose and a saviour. It helped to pull me through some of the darkest days of my life. For months I wanted to hide and become invisible. I shut the world away. My darkness was engulfing me and I could not see any light. On one of these dark days, my lovely husband Amit suggested I try baking again. Cocooned in my home kitchen, I gradually immersed myself in the world of baking, learning as much as I could. It kept me occupied: I had something to focus on.

Many times, the smoke alarm went off or the cake didn't go to plan! But it didn't matter. It was as if someone had switched the lights on. I was on a journey to learn everything I could, and I did not want to give up.

Over time, my confidence grew and, with encouragement from my friends and family, I started a small baking business – one that I still run from my home kitchen today. In 2011, for our tenth (tin) anniversary, Amit gifted me a domain name: Mylittlecaketin. He told me that this gift, named after that chapati tin from my childhood, was 'to create your own happiness, with a purpose'.

As a self-taught baker, I didn't have many reference points when I started. For me, there were no family recipes to fall back on. Most of my friends and family used the oven as storage! So, I started reading and collecting cookbooks. And whenever I came across memorable bakes or flavours while out and about, I found myself scribbling notes on napkins. Back at home, I would try to recreate them in my kitchen. Collecting recipes and learning about cakes became an obsession.

My methods, techniques and flavours may not be traditional – after all, I didn't have a map to start with – but through these pages, I humbly attempt to take you on my journey of baking knowledge, cake styles and flavours. Here, you will find my most-baked, most-loved and most-requested recipes from over the years.

If you are new to baking, welcome. There is so much joy to be found here. Don't be embarrassed to start simple: with a little time, love and perseverance, I know you will come to love the process as much as I do.

If you are a keen cake baker, I hope this book gives you a new perspective. May we share our love for baking to eternity.

To all my readers: recipes live only when they travel from one hand to another. I hope that some of these will find a regular space at your family table, and I hope they will inspire you to experiment, tweak, and to create your own recipes.

Baking found me in the darkest phase in my life. It has been my light ever since and provided me with moments of joy, stability and focus, and it continues to do so. I hope it brings you lots of happiness too.

Happy baking,
Tarunima

A love letter to flowers

Flowers have always been a part of my life. If you are familiar with my cakes, you will know that they have long been instrumental to my cake-making journey, too.

As a little girl back in India, my parents' garden was my sanctuary. My parents nurtured me and my love for flowers in the most tender way. I would spend hours tending to that garden, picking flowers for Ma's morning prayers, making garlands with my sisters, guarding the blooms from the cricket ball of my brother and his friends. It was, and still is, my happy place.

Flower-arranging had a place in my sleepy Indian town. I would take part in competitions and often win the prizes. Papa would drive me miles, always making time in his busy schedule because it also made him happy.

The aromas wafting throughout Indian festivals, too, carried a floral note: rose, saffron, marigold and jasmine all found their way into flavourings and decorations.

When I moved to London, flowers brought a continuity of sorts. Tending my garden here evokes memories of the home I left behind, and brings a promise of flowers to the home I share with my husband.

When I began my cake business from my little home kitchen, I knew I wanted my cakes to be colourful, vibrant and happy-looking, but I didn't know how. Then, one year, I placed some fragrant roses from my garden on a friend's birthday cake. From there it started, and it has only grown since.

In these pages, I humbly share everything I have learned while using edible flowers in the hope that you, too, will fall in love with them.

How this book works

This book is a collection of recipes, stories and memories I have accumulated through the years.

More than that, it is the book I wish I had when I started baking. I had no blueprint for making cakes, so here I have endeavoured to share everything I have learned, from ingredients and equipment to essential techniques and fundamental recipes, including all my most-loved cakes.

I encourage you to experiment with my recipes and add your own twists, making them even better as you go, to bring an extra dose of magic to your kitchen.

As you bake, I recommend you keep a journal, a dedicated notebook where you can note down oven timings and temperatures, flavour combinations and your own alterations, to always refer back to.

About the tin

The old chapati tin from which the 'Mylittlecaketin' name comes – the very tin you see photographed here – was 8 inches (20cm) in diameter, and probably more than 70 years old.

I now know that when it comes to baking, the size of the tin is very important. Adapting a recipe for a different sized tin is risky, and after all the effort you put in, wasting your time and ingredients is so disappointing.

Earlier on my baking journey, I would pick up a book, see that the recipe called for a tin I didn't have, and decide not to bake it to avoid disappointment.

So I thought: how great would it be to have a book where all the recipes use one standard-sized tin, with no need to adapt recipes or buy new equipment?

My book is a sincere attempt to carry that idea forward. I believe the 8-inch cake tin is the most versatile, hardworking tin in our kitchens, and that is the tin that features in all of these recipes.

On page 22 you'll find more information about types of tins and which will be best-suited to your baking needs.

The building blocks

This chapter covers the foundations of baking, starting with the ingredients and equipment you will need, followed by the techniques and fundamental recipes you will use throughout the book.

Make space in your day and put on your apron, and please allow me to guide you through the essentials, so you can bake with confidence and joy.

The best part of baking is that there is cake at the end: make sure you save a slice for yourself, always.

Ingredients

Essentials

Ingredients vary from season to season and from country to country – it can be confusing to know what we need, how to source it, and how to start building a baking pantry.

The foundations of a cake are flour, sugar, eggs, butter, dairy and a raising agent. Two other essentials for me are fine sea salt and good vanilla (see page 18). Everything else depends on your tastes, preferences, the seasons and availability. Start by allocating a space to your baking supplies. This way, you can keep an eye on it and replace things often.

There is no one list of ingredients that will suit all, so build yours in a way that suits you. If you are an occasional baker or just starting out, buy ingredients in small quantities to keep them fresh.

Note: All recipes use unsalted butter, whole (full-fat) milk, fine sea salt and free-range, medium eggs, unless otherwise stated.

Use all ingredients at room temperature, unless otherwise stated. Get them out of the fridge well before you begin – a couple of hours is best. Test this by pressing your finger into the butter: it should leave a clear indent and not be oily to the touch.

Flour

Plain (all-purpose) white flour: the base for most of the bakes, good-quality, freshly milled flour is best, but basic supermarket flour works too.

Self-raising flour: buy it or make your own by sifting 1 tsp baking powder into every 100g (¾ cup) plain flour.

Cake flour: cake flour is not readily available from supermarkets, but creates a lighter, superfine, milled flour. You can make your own by sifting cornflour (cornstarch) with plain flour: add 15g (about 2 Tbsp) cornflour to every 100g (¾ cup) plain flour.

Gluten-free flour: it's best to use a high-quality gluten-free flour. Not all raising agents are gluten-free – buying self-raising gluten-free flour means sourcing one less ingredient. I use Doves Farm self-raising flour as it gives consistent results.

Sugar

Caster (superfine) sugar: this type of sugar is essential for a good crumb. Golden caster sugar has a richer flavour than plain white caster sugar and I believe it enhances my baking, but it can be substituted 1:1 with white caster sugar in all of the recipes, if that's what you have to hand.

Soft light brown sugar and dark brown (muscovado) sugar: this adds rich caramel notes to the bakes, especially good in autumn baking and chocolate cakes.

Demerara (raw brown) sugar: a coarse-grain sugar, this is brown in colour, and does not melt during baking. I sprinkle it on everyday cakes to get a crunchy top, or add to crumbles.

Icing (confectioners') sugar is mostly used for decoration, glazes and American-style buttercream.

Eggs

Always use fresh, free-range and the best quality you can buy. Rich yellow yolks add a beautiful, rich, golden colour, especially to simple sponges. If your kitchen is very cold, you may find it helps to immerse your eggs in tepid water for 15 minutes before use.

Butter

There is no substitute for the flavour of good butter. A European-style butter with a high fat content – around 80 per cent – is worth paying extra for.

It's important to use room-temperature butter: if it is too warm, it will make the cake greasy. If your kitchen is too cold for it to soften, try grating it.

Milk and cream

Soured cream, **buttermilk**, **full-fat (whole) milk**, **yogurt** and **double (heavy) cream** are regularly used in my baking.

Soured cream: this adds a lot of moisture and extra fat to the cake and provides a good open, moist crumb.

Buttermilk: generally used with bicarbonate of soda (baking soda) in a recipe as they react to give a good crumb texture.

If you are unable to source soured cream or buttermilk, you can achieve a similar taste by adding 2 Tbsp lemon juice per 100ml (7 Tbsp) milk or cream and leaving it for 15 minutes to slightly curdle.

Make sure your ingredients aren't too cold as this stops dairy from emulsifying well. They may also curdle your batter, also resulting in a dense and an uneven cake crumb.

Vanilla

If you only take one thing away from this book, it is this: please use good vanilla. It enhances the flavour of any cake, even chocolate, and masks the smell and taste of the eggs. Avoid artificial vanilla flavouring and use real vanilla bean where you can. High-quality bean pods are expensive, so use the next best thing: vanilla bean paste, which has specks of vanilla bean, or good-quality vanilla extract.

Sea salt

Perhaps unexpectedly, salt balances the flavour and enhances the taste of batters, syrups, buttercream, jams – everything. Please, use it. The smallest amount truly makes all the difference.

I use Maldon sea salt flakes crushed into a fine powder. You can also buy ready-to-use fine sea salt. If you only have table salt, add with caution: it is sharper and stronger so you will need less than the amount stated.

Raising agents

Baking powder and **bicarbonate of soda (baking soda)** are important ingredients for all kinds of baking. Cake recipes often call for one or both. The quantities may be small but do not underestimate the importance of precision. Use measuring spoons and always level the spoon. Adding too much or too little can make a huge difference to your bake, causing the cake to dome or sink.

Always use fresh raising agents: opened tubs will start to lose their potency within 6 months. To test your baking powder or bicarbonate of soda, add a spoonful to a cup of hot water. If it fizzes, it's good to use.

Extras

The following extras will add interest, flavourings and seasonality to your bakes. Build your baking pantry to your own preference, and at your own pace.

Spices

Spices are flavour-enhancers: they are potent and should be used with consideration. Used correctly, they add so much flavour and elevate any bake, but add too much and it will overpower. The only way to build confidence with spices is to use them often. If you're new to this, take notes of your preferences as you learn.

It is important to use fresh spices as they can go stale. Unfortunately, spices are often wasted. Purchase as much as you will use, or buy whole spices and grind them fresh. If you do not use spices often, store them in airtight containers in the freezer. That way, they are convenient but last longer than in your cupboards. Similarly, buy spices for festive baking in small quantities to avoid wastage.

For the sake of flavour, even if you mostly use ground spices, please always use whole green cardamom pods, whole nutmeg and good-quality saffron strands.

Chocolate

I recommend you buy good-quality, fairtrade chocolate for batters and to decorate (page 51). I mostly use 70% **dark chocolate**, but if you prefer yours less dark, I suggest 50–55% cocoa.

Milk chocolate alone can be too sweet so I often use a combination of dark and milk chocolate.

White chocolate divides people, but it is a good ingredient to have as it adds depth and flavour to cake sponges. It is easy to overheat in the microwave so always melt in a heatproof bowl over a pan of gently simmering water. If you like, you can caramelize it for a couple of hours in a 100°C fan/120°C/250°F/ Gas mark ½ oven before using: it develops a rich caramel note that I really enjoy.

I use **Dutch-processed cocoa powder** for all my baking. You can use any unsweetened cocoa powder but do not confuse it with drinking chocolate, which is made with added milk and sugar.

Nuts

Nuts add flavour, texture and moisture to cakes, keeping them soft for a few extra days. They're also good for gluten-free baking. If you only use them occasionally, keep them in the freezer to stop them going rancid.

Pistachios

Unsalted pistachios: I use these whole or chopped, or grind them into powders as needed. You can buy ready-ground pistachios or use a spice grinder to make your own.

Pistachio nibs: these vibrant green slivers are used for decoration and can be found online or in Middle Eastern grocery stores.

Pistachio paste: a green paste that adds a rich pistachio flavour and a hint of colour to cakes and buttercreams. You can find it online or in Italian delis.

Almonds

Whole almonds: I use unskinned, lightly toasted almonds, then prepare as required.

Ground almonds: find these in supermarkets or grind your own using a spice grinder. Ground almonds retain moisture and texture without altering the cake's flavour too much.

Flaked (slivered) almonds: used for toppings and to sprinkle on cake batter, adding texture and crunch.

Coconut (technically not a nut!)

Desiccated (shredded) coconut: used in batters and to finish and decorate cakes. In the UK, this tends to be unsweetened, but if you can only get sweetened and are using it in a batter, reduce the sugar by 50g (¼ cup).

Coconut chips or flakes: generally used for decoration.

Coconut milk, **coconut oil** and **coconut cream** are useful for coconut-based cakes and in vegan baking.

Citrus

Citrus fruits add so much flavour to bakes. Ensure you buy unwaxed fruits – you don't want to zest wax into your cakes! If in doubt, soak the fruit in hot water for 30 minutes and scrub the peel.

Blood oranges are beautiful, sweet in flavour and not very sharp.

Lemon zest improves the flavour of many bakes. Rubbing it with caster (superfine) sugar releases the oil and perfumes the sugar, which permeates through the bake.

A squeeze of **lemon juice** also adds flavour: always zest before squeezing the juice out, even if you're not using the zest right away, as you can store it in a small ziplock bag in the freezer.

Fruits, berries and flowers

Every month of the year brings new and delicious fruits and berries. My parents always taught me to eat with the seasons, for which I am grateful.

There are a few ways to make the most of seasonal produce all year round.

One way is by preserving: when fruits are in season and their flavour is at its best, I make jams, curds (page 48), marmalade and compôtes (page 47) to use in my cakes (or sometimes freeze the prepared fruit to do this later). Similarly, I make cordials and syrups from flowers and leaves to add flavour to my cakes (see page 56).

If you don't want to make your own, buy good-quality, locally-produced jams, compôtes and curds.

Frozen fruits and berries are generally picked in season so retain their flavour. They contain too much water for cake batters (with the exception of blueberries and cherries, which can be baked from frozen) but are perfect for compôtes and fillings.

Freeze-dried fruit powders add colour and flavour without diluting batters or buttercream – perfect as I don't use artificial colours or flavourings.

Tools and equipment

Tins

All cakes in this book can be achieved with just one 20cm (8in), 7–10cm (3–4in) deep cake tin. The extra tins are suggestions only, but will reduce the effort, time and steps you need to recreate some of the more involved recipes.

Light aluminium tins provide a more even bake than darker-coloured ones, which tend to overbake cakes. If you don't already have good-quality light tins, I recommend those from PME or Silverwood.

20cm (8in) diameter anodised aluminium cake tin

This is your go-to tin and the one that almost all the recipes in this book call for. If you're going to bake sandwich cakes or buttercream cakes regularly, two or three tins will make things easier. You can, however, use one tin and bake in batches, or even construct layer cakes from thin layers of sponge baked in a single tin.

20cm (8in) diameter springform cake tin

These tins have a clip on the side and a loose base, useful for mousses and cheesecakes, and are generally only available in dark metal. They help with unmoulding the cake and save unnecessary stress.

20cm (8in) diameter loose-bottom cake tin

Round and with a loose base, this tin makes it easy to push the cake out, ideal for delicate or top-heavy cakes.

Preparation

My early days in the kitchen were spent in India, where there is no concept of measuring when it comes to cooking! Over the years, though, I have learned to befriend my scales, thermometers and measuring tools.

Digital scales

A flat digital battery-operated scale is cheap, easy to store and absolutely essential. While the recipes give conversions by volume, I strongly recommend you measure your ingredients by weight.

Spatula

I don't know what bakers did before the silicone spatula was invented. I guess we all licked the bowls! A couple of good flexible ones will make the whole job easier and help scrape the bowl clean. I recommend keeping a pair aside only for sweet baking.

Pastry brush

A pastry brush is handy for buttering or oiling tins and brushing cakes with syrup. I prefer silicone but traditional pastry brushes work too.

Microplane grater

This may be considered a specialist tool but I highly recommend buying one. It's the absolute best tool for zesting citrus fruits and grating nutmeg. If you only have a box grater, the fine side will work for zesting to some extent.

Spice grinder

Although not essential, a spice grinder makes light work of grinding nuts and spices to use in your recipes. Alternatively, use a coffee grinder.

Large, medium and small bowls

It is worth having a couple of each size, even better if they are stackable for storage. Steel is best but glass, ceramic or plastic all work. If you have a stand mixer, I recommend buying an extra bowl for it.

Measuring spoon set

A must for measuring small quantities. Don't underestimate the value of this handy little set when it comes to baking and using precise measurements. And remember: always level your spoon.

Pans

You want a small and a medium heavy-based saucepan: these pans maintain an even cooking temperature, essential for brown butter, compôtes, syrups and custards.

Sieve (strainer)

A large metal sieve to sift flour, a nylon sieve to catch the seeds and skins of fruit when making purées and a fine tea strainer to sift icing (confectioners') sugar and powders are all useful to have in the kitchen.

Hand-held beater

This is a less expensive alternative to a stand mixer. It does the job of mixing batter and whipping cream (buy one that has a whisk attachment as well as beaters). It saves time – and some elbow grease. A must-have, if you intend to make cakes often.

Stand mixer

I love my stand mixer! It's like having a second pair of hands that does all the hard work. It is an expensive piece of equipment so a hand-held beater, above, will work fine if you only bake occasionally. If you are a keen baker, though, it is worth every bit of your hard-earned money and precious counter space.

Stand mixers are great for keeping your hands free. They also help with consistency.

Knives

No kitchen should be without a set of sharp knives. A heavy knife (for portioning cakes and chopping nuts), a small everyday knife (for chopping fruit), a long serrated knife (for slicing cakes horizontally), and a sturdy long-bladed palette knife (for buttercreams and fillings) are good investments.

Baking

A cake in the oven may be browned and risen but is it cooked in the middle? Understanding the smell, texture and feel are skills one should nurture, but in this section you will find aids that act as extra insurance.

Note: The recipes in this book are tested in a standard fan-assisted oven as that is what I use at home.

Almost all the cakes in this book are baked at 160–170°C fan (180–190°C/ 350–375°F/Gas mark 4–5).

Baking at this temperature yields less domed cakes and a more even bake. It may take longer at these temperatures, but I find that higher temperatures can make the cake rise too fast, browning it on top and producing dry edges while sometimes leaving it undercooked in the middle.

Eco-friendly baking paper

Lining the tin (see instructions on pages 26–7) avoids sticking and over-browning. You can find pre-cut 20cm (8in) discs online for conveniently lining the base.

Oven thermometer

Getting to know your oven is something I can't emphasize enough. All ovens vary: each has a cold and a warm side, and the internal temperature often differs to the one you have set it to. An oven thermometer can give a more reliable temperature reading.

If you don't have one, rotating the cake tin after three-quarters of the baking time has passed will ensure more even baking. Similarly, tenting the cake three-quarters of the way through baking time with a piece of foil helps to reduce over-browning.

Each time you bake a cake, it is worth noting down the temperature of your oven and the time it took for a skewer to come out clean.

Digital probe thermometer

Inexpensive and extremely useful, this little tool can help you in every step – from making caramels to Swiss meringue buttercream and even for using as a skewer to test whether a cake is done – if it comes out clean, your cake is ready. It takes away a lot of the guesswork and gives you the confidence to try things that felt out of reach before. Please buy one and make it your best friend in the kitchen.

Wire cooling rack

It is important to cool the cake on a wire rack to let the steam escape and prevent sogginess. Round or rectangle is fine, and having two wire racks is extra useful. It also helps when decorating a cake with melted chocolate or a warm glaze as the rack allows the excess to fall through – just place a large oven tray or a few layers of newspaper under the rack to catch the excess drips.

Assembly & decoration

In many respects this is the fun part but it takes practice, attention to detail and being present. These items will help make the process more efficient.

Eco-friendly cling film (plastic wrap)

Cling film is used for ease of assembly and unmoulding later, ideal for layered and filled cakes.

Turntable

If you are going to be decorating cakes a lot, a stable metal 30cm (12in) diameter turntable will make all the difference – I like Ateco. They are expensive but will be with you for years to come. For occasional use, a basic plastic one will suffice.

Metal cake or bench scraper

If your focus is on buttercream cakes, this tool helps you achieve neat finishes: I can't recommend it highly enough. If you are an occasional baker, you could start with a plastic one and upgrade later, if you like.

There are a few other useful items that may already be in your kitchen: a food processor, mini chopper, a stick (immersion) blender, a high-speed counter blender such as a Nutribullet and a bain-marie. You may have some of them already, or you can decide whether to invest in them.

Techniques

Sifting

Sifting the flour helps to aerate the mix and creates lighter cakes. I use a metal sieve (sifter) and always sift the flour together with the raising agents, salt and any spices or other dry ingredients like cocoa powder to distribute them evenly through the batter.

Adding eggs

Sometimes adding eggs curdles the batter, which scares many a home baker. Eggs have a high water content: trying to emulsify them with the high-fat creamed butter and sugar mixture is a difficult but crucial step in making cake batter.

Adding cold eggs may cause the batter to curdle so maintaining a consistent temperature helps.

Adding eggs too quickly can also cause curdling. I like to break the eggs into a small jug, gently whisk them with a fork and pour them in little by little in 3–4 goes, emulsifying the batter by beating after each addition.

Creaming, beating and whisking

Creaming or beating incorporates air into the batter, making it light and fluffy in texture and creamy-pale in colour. Start your machine at a slow to medium speed and finish on high.

Under- or over-beating results in unsatisfactory bakes, so it's crucial to follow the timings as given.

If you are beating by hand, add about 4–5 minutes to the timings, and place a damp tea (dish) towel under your bowl to prevent the bowl sliding on the counter.

Folding

Folding refers to gently incorporating the ingredients, using a large metal spoon or a spatula. Going in heavy-handed or folding too vigorously can deflate the batter, resulting in a heavy, dense cake. Folding the ingredients in 2–3 smooth, confident strokes will maintain volume and incorporate the ingredients.

Lining the tin

This is an important step when baking a cake, with few exceptions.

Start by lining the inside of the tin with butter and flour, then place a disc of baking paper in the base. Use butter to brush the base, then brush the sides of the tin with upwards strokes to make the cake rise higher. Dust with a tablespoon of flour, shake all around the tin, then invert it with a sharp tap to get rid of any extra flour.

If the recipe requires, line the sides as well as the base to stop the cake from over-browning. It is good practice for cakes that take longer to bake, as well as for 'naked-style' cakes where you want the cake's edges to be paler.

Some recipes require an overhang of baking paper as this helps with lifting delicate cakes out of the tin. To do this, butter and flour the tin, then scrunch up a sheet of baking paper and open it out.

Fit it into the tin allowing an overhang of 5–13cm (2–5in). To make it easier to handle, moisten the paper with water before scrunching.

Lining the cake tin with cling film (plastic wrap)

This is important when building layered cakes: it helps with unmoulding the assembled, chilled cake, maintains its freshness and avoids freezer burn. To do this, lightly grease the base and sides of the cake tin. Take 2 large sheets of cling film and double-line the tin, layering it to cover the base and sides and allowing an overhang of 3–4cm (1¼–1½in). Press it firmly and evenly on the sides and base.

Turning out of the tin

Once a cake is baked, it's important to let it cool for 10 minutes, still in the tin. If a recipe asks you to invert the cake, this means to turn the tin upside-down. Alternatively, turning the cake out of the tin means keeping it upright.

Cake construction and assembly

This section shows you how to assemble, layer, finish and build tiers, using one simple batter and the buttercream recipe from pages 52–3. There are even solutions for if your cake doesn't go to plan – see the cake truffles, overleaf.

Refer back to this section for a guide on how to finish your cake at every stage. You can also use it as a blueprint upon which to experiment and create your own bespoke flavour combinations.

The basic cake batter

You can confidently use this batter for any occasion. I started with the simplest of cakes and from there learned to make celebration cakes and even wedding cakes. You can too!

1 Butter and flour a 20cm (8in) round cake tin. Line the base with a disc of baking paper. Preheat the oven to 170°C fan/190°C/375°F/Gas mark 5.

2 Sift the flour, baking powder and salt into a bowl.

3 Break the eggs into a small jug and stir with a fork.

4 Put the butter and sugar in a large bowl, if using a wooden spoon or hand-held beater, or a stand mixer with a beater attachment, and cream until the mixture is pale and fluffy – this takes about 6–8 minutes. In this method, the creaming is the most important step.

5 Add the eggs in 3–4 goes, beating well after each addition. Add the vanilla and soured cream and mix well. Gradually add the flour mixture in 3–4 goes, folding in gently after each addition.

6 Pour the batter into the prepared tin. Tap the tin gently on the counter to release any air pockets. Bake for 35–40 minutes or until the surface is springy to touch and a skewer comes out clean.

7 Cool the cake for 10 minutes in the tin, then turn out onto a wire rack.

- 250g (1 cup plus 2 Tbsp) butter, plus extra for greasing
- 250g (1¾ cups plus 2 Tbsp) plain (all-purpose) flour, plus extra for dusting
- 1½ tsp baking powder
- ¼ tsp salt
- 5 eggs
- 250g (1⅓ cups plus 1 Tbsp) golden caster (superfine) sugar
- 1 Tbsp vanilla bean paste
- 75ml (¼ cup plus 1 Tbsp) soured cream

1   Everyday counter cake

Make this cake your own by adding spices, seasonal fruit and berries, nuts or citrus zests to the basic batter: the possibilities are endless.

---

1 Once the cake has cooled, cut it into small slices, then store in an airtight tin on the counter for 2–3 days and watch it disappear.

- 1 batch of Basic Cake Batter (page 28), baked and cooled

2   Mini cakes

Some days call for dainty little cakes like these – think of these as finger food for canapés or small bites to enjoy with afternoon tea. You just need a cookie cutter to stamp these out.

---

1 Place the completely cooled cake in the freezer for 20 minutes. (This is optional but chilling makes it easier to cut neater rounds.)

2 Stamp out rounds using a cookie cutter: a 5cm (2in) diameter will give about 10 mini cakes; 3cm (1¼in) diameter about 12–15 bite-size cakes. Save the offcuts to make cake truffles (see opposite).

3 Pipe buttercream or ganache on the tops and decorate as you wish.

- 1 batch of Basic Cake Batter (page 28), baked and cooled
- ¼ batch of Swiss Meringue Buttercream (pages 52–3)
- fruit, berries or nuts (optional)

Tips:

As the sponge sides are exposed, mini cakes will dry out quicker than a whole cake, so cut the rounds on the day they are required.

Cakes taste better freshly baked, but if you want to get ahead, bake one a few weeks in advance and freeze it, wrapped in cling film (plastic wrap). Defrost for an hour at room temperature and follow the steps as above.

3 Cake truffles

If your cake is overbaked, sunken or has broken, make cake truffles with it! Offcuts from the batch of mini cakes (see opposite) can also be used in this way. A whole cake will give 30–35 cake truffles; offcuts will yield about 12 – adjust your binding ingredients accordingly.

1 Crumble the cake into a bowl and add enough cream or spread to bind it. Whatever you choose, don't add too much: add a spoonful at a time, just enough to bind the crumbs into a soft dough. Use your hands to form small balls. Space your truffles out on a tray lined with baking paper and place in the freezer for 20 minutes.

2 Melt the chocolate and stir in the sunflower oil. Once the cake balls are frozen, dip them in the melted chocolate and place back on the tray. Sprinkle with nuts or flower petals, if using. Let the chocolate set, then put your truffles in petit four cases or arrange on a tray to serve.

- trimmed offcuts from mini cakes (opposite) or 1 batch of Basic Cake Batter (page 28), baked and cooled
- leftover cream, Buttercream (see pages 52–4), Ganache (page 51), chocolate spread or nut butter, to bind
- 100–200g (3½–7oz) chocolate, depending on how many truffles you have
- 1–2 tsp sunflower oil (one spoonful per 100g/3½oz chocolate)
- chopped nuts or edible flower petals (optional)

4 Single-layer cake

Sometimes you need a cake that's easy to assemble but looks special. Single-layer cakes are amazing for small celebrations as they can be dressed up or kept simple, as needed.

1 Once the cake has cooled, top it with the buttercream or whipped cream. Decorate with seasonal fruit or berries and edible flowers.

- 1 batch of Basic Cake Batter (page 28), baked and cooled
- ½ batch of Swiss Meringue Buttercream (pages 52–3) or 200ml (¾ cup plus 1 Tbsp) whipped cream
- seasonal fruit or berries and edible flowers (optional)

5 Sandwich (two-layer) cake

*This cake can be layered with buttercream or whipped cream
and/or jam, curd or fruit.*

---

1 Place one of the cake layers on a cake board or plate. Top
with the buttercream or whipped cream, spreading it with
the back of a spoon to make a little dam around the rim. Add
a few spoonfuls of jam or curd and fresh berries, if you wish.
Sandwich with the other cake layer. Dust with icing sugar and
decorate with edible flowers.

Tip:

You can follow the basic recipe and bake this in a 20cm (8in)
cake tin or, if you have two or even three tins this size, divide
the batter equally between them and reduce the baking time
to 24–26 minutes, or until a skewer comes out clean. This
saves on time in the oven and avoids the stress of horizontally
slicing the cake.

· 1 batch of Basic Cake Batter (page
  28), baked and cooled, then sliced
  horizontally into 2 discs (see page 34,
  or see tip)
· ½ batch of Swiss Meringue Buttercream
  (pages 52–3) or whipped cream
· jam (jelly) or Curd (page 48)
· fresh seasonal berries (optional)
· icing (confectioners') sugar, for dusting
· edible flowers (optional)

6 Three-layer naked cake

*Uncoated cakes, where the layers are visible, are known as bare or
naked cakes.*

---

1 Place one of the cake layers on a cake board or plate. Top
with the buttercream or whipped cream, spreading it with
the back of a spoon to make a little dam around the rim. Add
a few spoonfuls of jam or curd. Top with the second cake
layer. Repeat the process with the buttercream and jam. Top
with the third layer of the sponge. Pipe buttercream on top or
dust with icing sugar.

2 To serve, decorate with fruit, berries or edible flowers, if
you wish.

· 1 batch of Basic Cake Batter (page
  28), baked and cooled, then sliced
  horizontally into 3 discs (see page 34,
  or see tip above)
· ½ batch of Swiss Meringue Buttercream
  (pages 52–3)
· jam (jelly) or Curd (page 48)
· icing (confectioners') sugar, for dusting
· fresh seasonal fruit, berries or edible
  flowers (optional)

7 Semi-bare buttercream finish

Here, a very thin layer of buttercream or cream covers the outside of the assembled cake but the cake layers remain visible for a rustic finish.

1 Place one of the cake layers on a cake board or plate. Top with the buttercream, spreading it with the back of a spoon to make a little dam around the rim. Add a few spoonfuls of jam or curd, if you wish. Top with the second cake layer. Repeat the process with the buttercream and jam. Top with the third layer of the sponge.

2 Using a cake palette knife, spread a thin layer of buttercream all around the sides and top of the cake. This is known as the 'crumb coating'. Neaten the sides using a cake scraper (see below).

3 Place the cake in the fridge for about 1 hour. Once the cake has chilled, set it (still on the board) on a cake turntable. Apply another thin layer of the buttercream to the top and the sides of the cake. Smooth it again with a cake or bench scraper. The cake layers should still be visible, but with a neat finish.

4 Top with fresh rose petals or berries, if using.

How to use a turntable and cake scraper

Place your chilled cake, on its board, on a cake turntable. Cover the top and sides of the cake with a thick layer of buttercream. Now with your dominant hand, hold the scraper upright, so the long edge is perpendicular to the cake and the short side is anchored to the board. Slowly spin the turntable with the other hand, rotating a full 360 degrees. (The hand holding the scraper should be stationary: the turntable rotates the cake, which gives the clean finish.) Remove any excess buttercream that collects on the scraper: keep the scraper clean at all times. Fully rotate the turntable a couple more times to give a smooth finish.

- 1 batch of Basic Cake Batter (page 28), baked and cooled, then sliced horizontally into 3 discs (see page 34, or see tip opposite)
- ½ batch of Swiss Meringue Buttercream (pages 52–3)
- jam (jelly) or Curd (page 48)
- rose petals or fresh berries (optional)

8 Full buttercream finish

This finish is for a fully coated cake. Using a turntable and a cake scraper helps ensure a beautifully smooth result.

---

1 Follow the method for the semi-bare buttercream finish on page 33 to fill and assemble your cake to the crumb coating stage. Use a cake scraper to go round the cake and neaten the sides. Place the cake in the fridge for about 1 hour. Once the cake has chilled, set it (still on the board) on a cake turntable. Cover the top and sides of the cake with a thick layer of the buttercream, then use the cake scraper again to achieve a smooth finish with no gaps.

2 Place the cake in the fridge to chill for 2–3 hours (or 6–8 if you need it to travel). To serve, decorate the cake with fresh or dried edible flowers.

- 1 batch of Basic Cake Batter (page 28), baked and cooled, then sliced horizontally into 3 discs (see below, or see tip on page 32)
- 1 batch of Swiss Meringue Buttercream (pages 52–3)
- fresh or dried edible flowers, to decorate

Building tiers

To build a tier, it is important that the sponge cakes are sturdy and the fillings the right texture and temperature to carry the layers. As with the construction of a building, you need to get the foundations and materials right before attempting to tier. The Basic Cake Batter (page 28) and either Swiss Meringue Buttercream (pages 52–3) or the Ganache on page 51 are ideal for this. Never tier using delicate cake sponges, such as chiffon or fat-free sponges, or using fresh cream fillings – they are not strong enough to hold the cakes up.

Also of real importance in preventing a tiered cake from collapsing is the internal support, which bears the weight of the top cake. This comes in the form of either plastic or wooden dowels (buy online or in cake shops), or you can use thick bubble tea straws, which are also widely available.

Cutting cakes

When cutting cakes, I find it helpful to insert toothpicks all around the cake, as pictured, to guide me. Then, using a serrated knife, slice with a gentle sawing motion, rotating the cake as you go to get even layers. You can slice cakes into 2, 3 or more layers this way. You may find it helps to use a flat cake lifter to move them as they will be fragile.

9 Two-tier cake

*Stacking cakes gives an immediate wow factor. With a little bit of
practice and confidence you can use the basic cake batter to create
a tiered cake for a celebration or even a small wedding cake. Allow
yourself plenty of time to tier the cakes – they must be completely
chilled before you begin.*

1 Prepare both cakes to the full buttercream finish stage (see
opposite). Before starting to tier the cakes, make sure they
have been well chilled (6–8 hours, or 24 hours if you need it to
travel). Sit both cakes on 20cm (8in) round cake drums.

2 Place one of the chilled cakes on a cake stand that will be
able to take the weight of both cakes. (If in doubt, use a large
metal plate or a wooden chopping board, because some cake
stands are flimsy and these cakes are heavy.)

3 Once the cake is secure on the stand or board, insert 6 cake
dowels or bubble tea straws into the top of the cake, pushing
them down to the base of the cake. Make sure the dowels are
spaced equally and well apart from each other, as they carry
the weight of the second cake. If using straws, use sharp
scissors to snip off the excess to make them level with the
top of the cake. If using wooden dowels, measure the height
of the cake and cut the length of the dowels to match using a
serrated knife or scissors.

4 Put 2–3 tablespoons of the buttercream on top of the cake,
spreading it slightly. The extra buttercream helps to secure
the cakes.

5 Take the second chilled cake from the fridge and carefully
place it on top of the dowelled cake, still on its drum. Make
sure the cakes are aligned.

6 Finish and decorate the cake with edible flowers.

7 To easily portion cakes into small, neat slices, first chill
the cake well. Then, using a large knife, divide the cake into
horizontal slices, then repeat vertically.

Variation

The method here makes what is called a double-barrel cake.
You can also make a staggered tiered cake by having the top
cake smaller. Simply trim the second 20cm (8in) cake to a
diameter of 15cm (6in) and use the offcuts to make cake truffles
(see page 31). When placing the dowels in the bottom cake,
position them only within the radius of the smaller top cake.

- 2 batches of Basic Cake Batter (page
  28), baked and cooled, then sliced
  horizontally into 3 discs (see opposite,
  or see tip on page 32)
- 2 batches of Swiss Meringue Buttercream
  (pages 52–3)
- edible flowers (optional)

The basic batters

There are many methods for producing a cake batter, which all result in different crumbs and structures, suitable for different types of cakes. Keeping the ingredients and flavours almost identical helped me in my early baking days to understand texture, flavour and crumb.

Return to this chapter in your own time to gain a better understanding of the process, or use it as a base to experiment with flavour.

As you practise, start getting to know your oven: note down the time and temperature for next time.

All-in-one method

This method is the easiest: I recommend it if you are new to baking, are baking with kids or are short of time. It is mess-free and practically stress-free. You simply weigh the unshelled eggs and use the same weight of flour, sugar and butter, then mix all the ingredients in one. As a guide, 4 whole unshelled eggs are usually 185–190g (about 6½oz).

Difficulty: Very easy

Uses: As Victoria sponge, layered with jam (jelly) or buttercream

Prep time: 5 minutes

1 Butter and flour a 20cm (8in) round cake tin. Line the base with a disc of baking paper. Preheat the oven to 170°C fan/190°C/375°F/Gas mark 5.

2 Put all the ingredients in a large bowl, if using a wooden spoon or a hand-held beater, or a stand mixer with a beater attachment. Beat for 3–4 minutes, or until you have a pale and fluffy batter that is fully combined.

3 Pour the batter into the prepared cake tin. Tap the tin gently on the worktop to release any air pockets. Bake for 35–40 minutes, or until the surface is springy to touch and a skewer comes out clean.

4 Cool the cake for 10 minutes in the tin, then turn out onto a wire rack.

- 185g (¾ cup plus 1 Tbsp) butter, plus extra for greasing
- 185g (1⅓ cups) plain (all-purpose) flour, plus extra for dusting
- 4 eggs
- 185g (1 cup plus 1 tsp) golden caster (superfine) sugar
- 1 tsp vanilla extract
- ½ tsp salt
- 1½ tsp baking powder
- 4 Tbsp milk

Creaming

This is the classic, tried-and-tested method for cake batter, which starts with creaming butter and sugar, then folding in the remaining ingredients to avoid losing the air incorporated while creaming. This method gives a better crumb texture than the all-in-one method, and it's versatile – extra ingredients can simply be added to the basic batter.

Difficulty: Simple

Uses: Basic sponge to top with cream and fruit, or can be layered up for birthday and wedding cakes

Prep time: 15 minutes

1 Butter and flour a 20cm (8in) round cake tin. Line the base with a disc of baking paper. Preheat the oven to 170°C fan/190°C/375°F/Gas mark 5.

2 Sift the flour, baking powder and salt into a bowl.

3 Break the eggs into a small jug and stir with a fork.

4 Put the butter and sugar in a large bowl, if using a wooden spoon or hand-held beater, or a stand mixer with a beater attachment. Cream until the mixture is pale and fluffy – this takes about 6–8 minutes with electric beaters. Here, the creaming is the most important step.

5 Add the eggs in 3–4 goes, beating well after each addition. Add the vanilla and mix well. Gradually add the flour mixture in 3–4 goes. Stir in the milk. The mixture should have a dropping consistency.

6 Pour the batter into the prepared tin, then level the surface. Tap the tin gently on the worktop to release any air pockets. Bake for 35–40 minutes, or until the surface is springy to touch and a skewer comes out clean.

7 Cool the cake for 10 minutes in the tin, then turn out onto a wire rack.

- 200g (¾ cup plus 2 Tbsp) butter, plus extra for greasing
- 250g (1¾ cups plus 2 Tbsp) plain (all-purpose) flour, plus extra for dusting
- 1 tsp baking powder
- ¼ tsp salt
- 4 eggs
- 200g (generous 1 cup) caster (superfine) sugar
- 1 tsp vanilla extract
- 3 Tbsp milk

Variation: Brown butter method

1 Replace the butter with the same amount of Brown Butter (see page 46), and swap the caster sugar for the same amount of soft brown sugar. You can also add 100g (3½oz) toasted chopped pecans, if you like.

Reverse creaming method

This little-known method took me by surprise when I came across it many years ago, but it has become one of my preferred ways of making a sponge. It gives a tender, delicate crumb but a slightly dense texture – not in a negative way – and somehow it tastes richer and more buttery than other methods. It's key here not to overmix the batter.

Difficulty: Simple

Uses: Good for everyday cakes, topped with cream and berries

Prep time: 10 minutes

1 Butter and flour a 20cm (8in) round cake tin. Line the base with a disc of baking paper. Preheat the oven to 170°C fan/190°C/375°F/Gas mark 5.

2 Sift the flour, sugar, baking powder and salt into a large bowl if using a hand-held beater, or a stand mixer with a beater attachment. Give everything a quick mix. Add the butter. Beat until the mixture has a sandy breadcrumb-like texture.

3 Put the cream, eggs and vanilla in a small jug and whisk with a fork. Pour the mixture into the bowl in 3–4 goes, mixing well after each addition.

4 Pour the batter into the prepared tin. Tap the tin gently on the worktop to release any air pockets. Bake for 40–45 minutes, or until the cake starts to shrink from the sides of the tin and a skewer comes out clean.

5 Cool the cake for 10 minutes in the tin, then turn out onto a wire rack.

- 200g (¾ cup plus 2 Tbsp) butter, cut into cubes, plus extra for greasing
- 200g (1½ cups) plain (all-purpose) flour, plus extra for dusting
- 200g (generous 1 cup) golden caster (superfine) sugar
- 1½ tsp baking powder
- ½ tsp salt
- 100g (scant ½ cup) soured cream
- 4 eggs
- 1 tsp vanilla extract

Wet and dry method

This method combines a wet and a dry mix to form the batter, and the best part is you don't need any special equipment.

Growing up in India, we did not have caster sugar so we would blitz granulated sugar, which has larger crystals, to the consistency of icing sugar. I sometimes still use icing sugar as it results in a fine, delicate crumb. We would also use sunflower oil, not butter, as it was too expensive. Here I include both because butter adds so much more flavour.

Difficulty: Medium

Uses: Good for everyday cakes or filled with cream or buttercream, or can be left for a few days, then soaked and used as a trifle base

Prep time: 10 minutes

1 Butter and flour a 20cm (8in) round cake tin. Line the base with baking paper. Preheat the oven to 160°C fan/180°C/350°F/Gas mark 4.

2 Sift the dry ingredients into a large bowl.

3 Add the melted butter, oil, milk and vanilla to a separate large bowl and stir together. Add the eggs to this wet mixture and mix well with a fork.

4 Pour the wet ingredients into the dry ingredients. Using a large wooden spoon or spatula, mix together to a smooth batter.

5 Pour the batter into the prepared tin. Tap the tin gently on the worktop to release any air pockets. Bake for 35–40 minutes, or until the surface is springy to touch and a skewer comes out clean.

6 Cool the cake for 10 minutes in the tin, then turn out onto a wire rack.

- 200g (¾ cup plus 2 Tbsp) butter, melted, plus extra for greasing
- 300g (2¼ cups) plain (all-purpose) flour, plus extra for dusting
- 1½ tsp baking powder
- 300g (2 cups plus 2 Tbsp) icing (confectioners') sugar (or make your own – see recipe intro)
- ½ tsp salt
- 75ml (5 Tbsp) sunflower oil
- 100ml (7 Tbsp) milk
- 1 Tbsp vanilla bean paste
- 4 eggs

Genoise sponge method

I love to make layered cakes using this method. It has no chemical raising agent to make the cake rise, instead relying on air incorporated by vigorously whisking the eggs and sugar. The batter is more fluid and lighter than the others in this section and generally poured into the tin like liquid. This method takes time and practice, but you will love the delicate crumb and soft texture of Genoise, once you have mastered it.

Difficulty: Medium

Uses: Layered with fresh cream or buttercream

Prep time: 25 minutes

1 Butter (or oil) and flour a 20cm (8in) round cake tin. Line the base with a disc of baking paper and line the sides with more paper to come a little higher than the tin. Preheat the oven to 160°C fan/180°C/350°F/Gas mark 4.

2 Sift the flour, cornflour and salt into a bowl.

3 Put the eggs and sugar in a large glass or metal bowl, if using a hand-held whisk, or the metal bowl of a stand mixer. Place the bowl on a pan of barely simmering water (ensure the base of the bowl does not touch the water) over a medium-low heat. Stir continuously for 7–8 minutes. The sugar has dissolved when you can no longer feel the grains between your fingers.

4 Remove from the heat and, using a whisk attachment, whisk on medium speed for 3–5 minutes, or until the mixture is becoming paler and thicker. Increase the speed to high and keep whisking for 5–7 minutes. By now the mixture will have trebled in volume and become airy and very pale. When you lift the whisk, it should leave a trail of mixture, resembling ribbons, on the surface of the batter. This is known as the 'ribbon stage' and is crucial to this method.

5 Very gently but quickly sift the dry ingredients into the batter (this is the second sift, to keep the cake airy), then fold in using a large metal spoon or spatula in 3–4 goes, until they are well combined and no flour streaks remain. Try not to deflate the batter.

- 50g (3½ Tbsp) butter, melted, or sunflower oil, plus extra for greasing
- 175g (1⅓ cups) plain (all-purpose) flour, plus extra for dusting
- 25g (¼ cup) cornflour (cornstarch)
- ¼ tsp salt
- 6 eggs
- 200g (generous 1 cup) golden caster (superfine) sugar
- 1 tsp vanilla extract

6 Add the melted butter or oil to a small bowl. Add 2–3 tablespoons of the batter and the vanilla, and mix it well. Pour this into the remaining batter and very gently fold it in. Mix as gently and quickly as possible: overmixing will make a dense and flat sponge.

7 Pour the batter into the prepared tin. Tap the tin gently on the worktop to release any air pockets. Bake for 40–45 minutes – though it may need a little longer – or until the surface is springy to touch and a skewer comes out clean.

8 Cool the cake for 10 minutes in the tin, then invert it onto a wire rack, still in the tin, and let it cool completely before peeling off the paper.

Tip:

If unsure, very slightly overbake the cake as it can be brushed with sugar syrup and cream fillings. Underbaked and it will be of no use!

Joconde sponge method

Joconde sponges are used in thin layers in French gâteaux and tend not to be baked at home. However, this is a good make-ahead cake as it includes ground almonds, which keep well. It is also good in cakes that benefit from chilling. The cake is baked on the dry side, then moistened with a sugar or fruit syrup or a milk soak. I am no pastry chef – this method works for my home-style bakes.

Difficulty: Medium

Uses: Layer cakes, fresh cream cakes and gâteaux

Prep time: 20 minutes

---

1 Butter and flour a 20cm (8in) round cake tin. Line the base with a disc of baking paper. Preheat the oven to 160°C fan/180°C/350°F/Gas mark 4.

2 Sift the flour, ground almonds and salt into a bowl.

3 Put the egg whites in a large bowl if using a hand-held beater, or in a stand mixer with a whisk attachment. Whisk for 2 minutes on medium speed. Add half the sugar, little by little, to the bowl, whisking for 7–8 minutes on medium-high speed until soft peaks form.

4 In a separate bowl, whisk the egg yolks and the rest of the sugar for 4–5 minutes, or until pale and fluffy. Add the flour mixture in 3–4 goes, using a large metal spoon or spatula to fold it in after each addition until fully combined. Add the vanilla. Spoon the meringue into the batter in 3–4 goes, folding it in gently after each addition, until well combined. Then slowly whisk in the melted butter.

5 Pour the batter into the prepared tin. Tap the tin gently on the worktop to release any air pockets. Bake for 40–45 minutes, or until the cake starts to shrink from the sides of the tin and a skewer comes out clean.

6 Cool the cake for 10 minutes in the tin, then turn out onto a wire rack.

- 25g (1¾ Tbsp) butter, melted, plus extra for greasing
- 100g (¾ cup) plain (all-purpose) flour, plus extra for dusting
- ¼ tsp salt
- 100g (1 cup) ground almonds
- 4 eggs, separated
- 100g (generous ½ cup) golden caster (superfine) sugar
- 1 tsp vanilla extract

Chiffon cake method

This method is generally used for Asian-style cream cakes. The sides of the cake tin are not greased or floured, which means the tin holds the batter and helps it to rise. This is a complex baking method but the result is the most delicate crumb and light, airy sponge. I like to make mine with flavourless oil, not butter.

Difficulty: Hard

Uses: Asian-style cream cakes

Prep time: 20 minutes

1 Lightly grease the base of a 20cm (8in) cake tin (not the sides) and line the base and sides with baking paper. Preheat the oven to 170°C fan/190°C/375°F/Gas mark 5.

2 Sift the flour, cornflour, baking powder and salt into a bowl.

3 Mix together the vanilla, milk and oil in a small jug.

4 Put the egg whites in a large bowl, if using a hand-held whisk, or a stand mixer with a whisk attachment, and whisk on medium-high speed for 2–3 minutes. Then add half the sugar, a tablespoon at a time, and whisk until stiff peaks form.

5 Put the egg yolks and the remaining sugar into another large bowl. Whisk for about 4–5 minutes, on medium speed, until the mixture is pale and thick.

6 Pour the vanilla, milk and oil into the egg yolk mixture in a thin stream. Gently fold in using a large metal spoon until well combined. Sift in the dry ingredients in 3–4 goes (this is the second sift, to keep the cake airy), again folding in gently.

7 Add 3–4 tablespoons of the meringue to the batter. Fold it in, then add the remaining meringue in 2–3 goes. Try not to deflate the batter and fold in gently until no streaks of egg white are visible.

8 Pour the batter into the prepared tin. Tap the tin gently on the counter to release any air pockets. Bake for at least 45 minutes, or until the surface is springy to touch and a skewer comes out clean.

9 Invert the cake tin onto a wire rack and leave the cake to cool completely, still in the tin. Once cooled, use a butter knife around the edge of the sponge to release it from the tin.

- 75ml (5 Tbsp) sunflower oil, plus extra for greasing
- 175g (1⅓ cups) plain (all-purpose) flour
- 25g (¼ cup) cornflour (cornstarch)
- 1 tsp baking powder
- ¼ tsp salt
- 1 tsp vanilla extract
- 100ml (7 Tbsp) milk
- 5 eggs, separated
- 200g (generous 1 cup) golden caster (superfine) sugar

Hot milk method

Pouring hot milk into batter sounds strange, but I assure you it works beautifully. This method yields a surprisingly tender cake, enriched with extra egg yolks, and is good for single-layer celebration cakes topped with whipped cream and seasonal fruits and berries.

---

1 Butter and flour a 20cm (8in) round cake tin. Line the base with baking paper. Preheat the oven to 170°C fan/190°C/375°F/Gas mark 5.

2 Sift the flour, baking powder and salt into a bowl.

3 Put the butter and milk in a small pan. Gently heat to a simmer until the butter has melted. Keep it simmering but do not boil.

4 Put the eggs, yolks, sugar and vanilla in a large bowl, if using a hand-held whisk, or a stand mixer with the whisk attachment. Beat on medium-high speed until the mixture is light and pale and has trebled in volume.

5 Add the flour mixture in 3–4 goes, gently folding it in without deflating the batter.

6 Put 5–6 tablespoons of the batter into a small bowl and pour in the hot milk and butter. Gently fold together: the batter will melt but it will also temper the mixture so that the hot liquid can be added to the remaining batter. Add this hot milk mixture to the bowl of cake batter, gently folding it in.

7 Pour the batter into the prepared tin. Tap the tin gently on the worktop to release any air pockets. Bake for 40–45 minutes, or until the surface is springy to touch and a skewer comes out clean.

8 Cool the cake for 10 minutes in the tin, then turn out onto a wire rack.

Difficulty: Medium

Uses: Single-layer cakes

Prep time: 15 minutes

- 100g (½ cup minus 1 Tbsp) butter, plus extra for greasing
- 220g (1⅔ cups) plain (all-purpose) flour, plus extra for dusting
- 2 tsp baking powder
- ¼ tsp salt
- 250ml (1 cup) milk
- 3 eggs plus 2 yolks (freeze the whites for another use)
- 340g (1¾ cups plus 2 Tbsp) golden caster (superfine) sugar
- 1 Tbsp vanilla bean paste

Fatless sponge method

For years, this cake was my nemesis. It is one of the most temperamental sponge methods so it needs practice, but, once mastered, it is like eating a cloud. It is perfect for summer, pairing well with fresh cream and berries. Ensure your egg whites are very fresh and make this cake when you have some time. Please don't give up if you struggle – it's definitely worth the effort!

This cake can also be baked in a bundt tin or tube pan, to make it easier to turn out – simply use a ring of baking paper instead of a disc.

Difficulty: Harder

Uses: Angel food cake

Prep time: 15 minutes

---

1 Lightly grease the base (not the sides) of a 20cm (8in) round cake tin and line with a disc of baking paper. Preheat the oven to 160°C fan/180°C/350°F/Gas mark 4.

2 Sift together the flour, cornflour, salt and half the sugar into a bowl.

3 Put the egg whites and cream of tartar in a large bowl if using a hand-held beater, or a stand mixer with a whisk attachment. Whisk together on medium speed for about 2 minutes. Add the remaining sugar, one spoon at a time, whisking on medium-high speed for about 8–10 minutes until soft peaks form. Add the vanilla.

4 Gently sift the dry ingredients into the meringue in 3–4 goes, using a large metal spoon or spatula to fold them in after each addition. Try not to deflate or overmix the batter: you need to work gently but quickly because this cake has no raising agent and relies on the air in the meringue.

5 Pour the batter into the prepared tin. Tap the tin gently on the worktop to release any air pockets. Bake for 45–50 minutes, or until the surface is springy to touch and a skewer comes out clean.

6 Cool the cake for 10 minutes in the tin, then invert the tin onto a wire rack and leave the cake upside down in the tin to cool completely. Once cooled, use a butter knife around the edge of the sponge to release it from the tin. It will be delicate but you can tease it out using gentle hand movements.

- butter or oil, for greasing
- 125g (1 cup minus 1 Tbsp) plain (all-purpose) flour
- 15g (about 2 Tbsp) cornflour (cornstarch)
- ½ tsp salt
- 225g (1 cup plus 2 Tbsp) golden caster (superfine) sugar
- 8 egg whites (save the yolks for custards etc. or they freeze well)
- 1½ tsp cream of tartar
- 1 Tbsp vanilla extract

Flavourings and fillings

Sometimes a cake needs a little something extra to make it that bit more special: a brush of syrup for moisture, or fillings of curd, jams and crème pâtissière for a sprinkling of joy, or brown butter – a total game changer.

Brown butter

Brown butter is one of the most loved ingredients in my kitchen, adding a rich, nutty flavour. It can be scaled up and stored in a sealed container in the fridge, then brought to room temperature or gently reheated as the recipe requires.

1 Put the butter in a small pan over a medium heat. Keep a close eye on it: it will melt and then start to foam. Slowly you will see dark residue settling in the base and clear golden liquid on top. Take care not to let it burn – an amber golden colour is good. Switch off the heat and strain into a suitable container.

Makes approx. 200g (¾ cup plus 2 Tbsp)

· 250g (1 cup plus 2 Tbsp) butter, cut into small cubes

Sugar syrup

Sugar syrup is used for adding moisture to layer cakes. You can also brush the syrup on cakes that feel a bit dry. I sometimes make a double batch for lemonade or cocktails.

1 Put the sugar, water and salt in a small pan over a medium to low heat. Let it simmer gently until all the sugar has dissolved. Turn off the heat and add the lemon juice. Store in a sterilized glass bottle, seal and keep in the fridge for a few weeks.

Makes approx. 250ml (1 cup)

· 250g (1¼ cups) granulated sugar
· 300ml (1¼ cups) water
· ½ tsp sea salt
· 1 Tbsp lemon juice

Basic compôte

I make compôtes using seasonal produce for cake fillings. This recipe uses blueberries, but to use other fruits simply weigh the fruit, then add half that weight in sugar, plus the zest of a lemon. Sugar is usually what sets a compôte but I add a cornflour–water paste to get away with using less.

1 Put the blueberries, sugar, lemon zest and juice and salt in a medium pan over a medium to low heat. Cook until the blueberries release some water and the sugar has dissolved. Stir the mixture so it does not stick to the bottom or burn. Continue to cook for about 10–15 minutes over a medium heat, squashing and breaking up the blueberries from time to time. Once they are mushy and the consistency has thickened, add the cornflour paste. Cook for a further 5 minutes, then turn off the heat.

2 Pour into sterilized glass bottles or suitable containers and leave to cool completely. The compôte will thicken further as it cools. Seal and store in the fridge for up to 5 days.

Makes approx. 300g (1 cup)

· 300g (about 2¼ cups) fresh blueberries
· 150g (¾ cup plus 1 Tbsp) golden caster (superfine) sugar
· zest and juice of 1 lemon
· ¼ tsp salt
· 1 tsp cornflour (cornstarch) mixed with 1 Tbsp water

Lemon curd

One of the most delicious fillings to make for cake, lemon curd is sharp and tangy, pairing well with lemon cakes, berries and fruits. A curd is somewhere between a custard in terms of consistency and jam in its usage.

This recipe works well using other citrus fruits, or with passion fruit or raspberry purée.

1 Place a small pan of water over a low heat.

2 Put the egg yolks in a medium heatproof bowl. Add the sugar and mix together using a balloon whisk for about 2 minutes until well combined. Add the lemon zest and juice and mix again.

3 Place the bowl on top of the pan of simmering water. The base of the bowl should not be in contact with the water. Keep the heat very low and constantly stir the mixture. You cannot leave it unattended, or cook over a high heat, or you will end up with scrambled eggs.

4 Once the mixture starts to thicken, which takes around 15–20 minutes, take the bowl off the heat. Add the butter, 1 or 2 cubes at a time, whisking after each addition, until all of the butter has been used. Stir in the salt.

5 Pass the curd through a fine sieve (strainer). Pour into sterilized glass jars or suitable containers and leave to cool completely.

6 Seal and store in the fridge for up to 10 days. Use as required.

Makes approx. 400ml
(1½ cups plus 3 Tbsp)

- 4 egg yolks
- 100g (generous ½ cup) golden caster (superfine) sugar
- zest of 4–6 large lemons and 100ml (7 Tbsp) freshly squeezed lemon juice
- 125g (½ cup plus 1 Tbsp) butter, cut into 2.5cm (1in) cubes
- ¼ tsp salt

Crème pâtissière

*Also known as pastry cream, crème pâtissière is a deliciously thick,
custardy filling for cakes and pastries, flavoured with vanilla.*

1 Put the milk, vanilla paste and about a third of the sugar in
a medium pan and bring to a gentle simmer over a medium
to low heat.

2 Put the egg yolks in a medium bowl with the remaining
sugar and sift in the cornflour. Using a balloon whisk, mix
until smooth and slightly paler in colour.

3 Remove the milk pan from the heat. Still whisking with one
hand, gently pour a third of the milk into the egg mixture.
This technique is known as tempering and it is used to bring
the two mixtures to a similar temperature, without the egg
yolks curdling.

4 Once mixed, pour the remaining milk into the bowl.
Mix thoroughly then pour the egg and milk mixture back
into the pan.

5 Place the pan back over a gentle heat and continuously
stir until the mixture starts to look like a thick custard and
is bubbling. This should take under 3–4 minutes, so keep
stirring to avoid it burning. Turn off the heat and add the
butter and salt. Stir until the butter has melted.

6 If the mixture has curdled, you can pass it through a fine
sieve (strainer) to remove any lumps. Pour into a suitable
container and place some cling film (plastic wrap) directly
on the surface of the custard. This prevents a skin forming on
the custard.

7 Leave for at least 3–4 hours to completely cool and set
before adding it to cream to make cake fillings. Crème
pâtissière can be prepared up to 3 days in advance and stored
in the fridge. Don't store it any longer, though, as the flavour
is better fresh.

Makes approx. 600–625g
(1lb 5oz–1lb 6oz), enough to fill
a three-layered 20cm (8in) cake

· 450ml (1¾ cups) milk
· 1 Tbsp vanilla bean paste
· 100g (generous ½ cup) golden caster
  (superfine) sugar
· 5 egg yolks (save the whites to make
  meringues or friands – see page 189)
· 15g (2 Tbsp) cornflour (cornstarch)
· 20g (1½ Tbsp) butter
· ¼ tsp salt

Decoration and finishes

After all the preparation, baking and then the washing up, decorating is both relaxing and rewarding. Whether you choose to decorate simply or with elaborate finishes, take pleasure in creating and give it your full attention.

Decorating requires practice, time and effort. The more you do it, the better the results. You don't need to stress or buy lots of decorating tools: start with the basics and let the design expression come naturally to you. Then, as you gain confidence, you can build on your techniques.

When baking for occasions, it's best to keep it at the level of decoration you feel confident with to avoid unneccessary stress or frustration.

For me, cake decorating is an instinctive process, but it was not always so. Like all good things, it took time and practice. Remember: design is nothing but a medium for your creativity. Use whatever brings you joy – or look to the colours, textures and shapes around you for inspiration. Be honest with it and have fun... always have fun.

A dusting of icing (confectioners') sugar

This finish hides many sins and requires no skill, only a tea strainer or a small fine-mesh sieve. Once the cake is completely cool, lightly sift icing sugar over the top. Do not dust a warm cake or the sugar will disappear! You can also dust with cocoa powder and freeze-dried fruit or berry powders.

For something fancier, you can lay a paper doily on the surface of the cake. Dust over the top, then gently lift the doily. Alternatively, you can use cookie cutter shapes like hearts, butterflies or animals: place the cutter on the surface and dust around it. Then remove it, leaving behind the impression of the cutter.

To incorporate edible flowers, sprinkle flowers and petals on top after dusting. This is one of my favourite ways to decorate: it's simple but yields instant results, and is guaranteed to make everyone call you 'star baker'.

Icing sugar drizzle

Take 250g (2 cups plus 2 Tbsp) of sifted icing sugar and mix it with 2 tablespoons of water, fruit juice or fruit purée to give you a thick coating consistency. Add the liquid a teaspoon at a time until the mixture reaches your desired consistency – be careful not to make it too thin. Finally, add a pinch of salt. If you like, add 1 or 2 tablespoons of freeze-dried berry powder for added flavour and colour. Store it in an airtight container or covered with a sheet of cling film (plastic wrap) until required. If it becomes too thick, add a teaspoon of hot water.

Chocolate

Chocolate can be used in many ways to finish a cake:

· Ganache is perfect for topping or completely coating a cake.

· Chocolate glaze is a great finish that sets firm.

· Melted chocolate can be drizzled over simple everyday cakes.

· Chocolate curls, chocolate shavings, chocolate shards or even shop-bought chocolates can be used to decorate.

Chocolate glaze

1 Add all the ingredients to a small saucepan over a medium heat. Heat, stirring continuously, until it is well combined and smooth, about 5–7 minutes.

2 Remove from the heat and keep it warm, at a pourable consistency. If it gets too thick, add a couple of spoonfuls of hot water and stir it back to the desired consistency.

· 150g (5¼oz) 55% dark chocolate, finely chopped

· 75g (about ½ cup) icing (confectioners') sugar

· 50ml (4 Tbsp plus 1 tsp) hot water

· 50g (about ½ cup) cocoa powder

· ¼ tsp salt

· 1 tsp vanilla extract

Chocolate ganache

1 Put the chopped chocolate in a medium bowl.

2 Gently heat the cream in a small pan at a gentle simmer. Do not boil.

3 Pour the hot cream into the chocolate. Leave for 5 minutes, then stir with a clean, dry spatula until it is glossy and smooth.

4 Once melted, stir in the butter, vanilla and salt. Stir until mixed in and the butter is melted.

5 Keep at room temperature until it thickens.

· 200g (7oz) milk chocolate, finely chopped

· 350ml (1¼ cups plus 2 Tbsp) double (heavy) cream

· 1 Tbsp butter

· ½ tsp vanilla extract

· pinch of salt

Swiss meringue buttercream

Swiss meringue buttercream involves several steps that require some care and attention, and you will need a digital probe thermometer. Don't be scared: step out of your comfort zone and you will be rewarded with the silkiest, most delicious, stable buttercream.

All of the buttercream cakes in this book use this buttercream as a base. Give it a go: this is my trusted recipe and I am sure you, too, will be happy with the results.

The eggs are gently cooked in the first step, meaning this recipe contains no raw egg and is safe to eat.

Before we begin, a few notes:

· Sometimes there is no substitute for time. Please do not rush.

· The ratio to make Swiss meringue buttercream is always 1:2:3, where egg white is 1, sugar is 2 and butter is 3.

· The process starts with making meringue. To make meringues for desserts, follow steps 1–4, then bake in the oven at 100°C fan/120°C/250°F/Gas mark ½ for 45–50 minutes. Alternatively, pipe into meringue 'kisses' and bake for 30 minutes.

· When adding butter to the meringue, the temperature of the butter is important: too warm and the buttercream will not whip properly and will not be stable enough. Too cold and it will *also* not whip properly, and may curdle. Both situations can be rescued, so please do not bin the mixture! See the tips, opposite.

1 Put the sugar and egg whites in a large, very clean metal or glass bowl. Place over a large pan of barely simmering water, making sure the base of the bowl does not touch the water.

2 Continuously stir the eggs and sugar, using a balloon whisk or spatula, over a gentle heat – you don't want scrambled eggs! This can take up to 8–10 minutes.

3 Use a digital probe thermometer to check when the temperature of the mixture reaches 70°C/158°F. If you don't have one, check whether the sugar has melted by feeling the mixture between your fingers. It should not feel gritty.

4 Turn off the heat and, using a hand-held whisk or the whisk attachment of a stand mixer, whisk the mixture on a low to medium speed for 3–4 minutes. Increase the speed to high and keep whisking for about 6–8 minutes more, until it has trebled in volume and is a white and glossy meringue, with medium peaks.

5 Change the whisk attachment for the beater attachment if using a stand mixer. Gradually beat the butter into the meringue on a medium to high speed, adding it little by little, incorporating after each addition. Keep whisking until all the butter has been added, for around 8–10 minutes. If it curdles slightly, keep whisking: it should come back together.

6 Once the buttercream is smooth, firm and glossy, add the vanilla bean paste and salt. Continue to whisk at a low speed, for a final 3–4 minutes, to get rid of any large air pockets and make it smoother for piping and decorating. The buttercream is now ready to use.

7 Swiss meringue buttercream is best when freshly made. However, you can make ahead and store it in the fridge for up to 3 days. When ready to use, let it come to room temperature completely.

Tips

· These days, cartons of pasteurised egg whites are readily available. Use them! There are 3 benefits: 1) they are already pasteurised and safe to use; 2) there are no wasted egg yolks; and 3) it is cheaper and more convenient. The best part is that they don't compromise on taste.

· **To remedy a very soft butter situation and a soft buttercream**, place the buttercream in the fridge for 30 minutes, then whisk again. It should then whisk to the right consistency. Keep placing in the fridge for a further 10–15 minutes, if needed, before whisking again.

· **To rescue a cold butter situation where the mixture has curdled**, put it back in the fridge for 30 minutes to return all the ingredients to a similar temperature. Then whisk it on a slow to medium speed and it should come together. If you still see bits of cold butter in the buttercream and the butter is not emulsifying, put a couple of spoonfuls of the buttercream in a small heatproof bowl. Place the bowl in a microwave for a few seconds until the buttercream has slightly melted. Then add this back to the buttercream bowl and mix together. Whisk on a low to medium speed for 5 minutes. This should fix the problem.

Makes enough to fill and cover a 20cm (8in) cake

· 400g (generous 2 cups) golden caster (superfine) sugar
· 200g (7oz) egg whites from approximately 4 eggs
· 600g (2⅔ cups) butter
· 1 Tbsp vanilla bean paste
· ½ tsp salt

American-style buttercream

I confess I don't often use American-style buttercream for my cakes but when I do need to use it, this is my trusted recipe. It is easy to make light and smooth, and not overly sweet. Any recipe in this book that calls for Swiss meringue buttercream can be made using this recipe, but note they will be slightly sweeter.

---

1 Put the butter in a large bowl if using a hand-held beater, or a stand mixer with a beater attachment. Beat on medium speed for 5–7 minutes until light and airy and almost doubled in volume. Slowly add the icing sugar a few tablespoons at a time, incorporating well after each addition. Keep beating until all the sugar has been incorporated. Increase the speed and beat for a further 8–10 minutes until the buttercream is pale and fluffy. Add the vanilla, cream and salt, reduce the speed and beat for a final 3–4 minutes. It is important to beat the buttercream slowly for the last few minutes to smooth out any large air pockets.

Makes enough to cover a 20cm (8in) cake

- 400g (1¾ cups) butter
- 350g (3 cups) sifted icing (confectioners') sugar
- 1 Tbsp vanilla bean paste
- 4 Tbsp double (heavy) cream
- 1 tsp salt

Edible flowers

Decorating with edible flowers is quick, easy and gives instant impact. Every recipe in this book can be decorated with edible flowers – dried, fresh or sugar-coated – if you like.

There are two categories of edible flower: culinary ingredients, used for flavour (see page 57), and decorative, which have little to no taste.

A note on safety

You **must** check that your flowers are edible and non-toxic before using them on your cakes. Even edible flowers are only fit for human consumption when they are pesticide-free, correctly prepared, hygienically handled and stored and correctly identified. Even so much as placing a toxic or inedible flower on a cake as decoration can spread toxic sap, pesticides or contaminated water to your food, making the cake no longer safe to eat. If you have any doubts whatsoever about a flower or its origin, **do not use it**.

It is also important to note that some edible flowers are not safe for some people to consume due to allergies (including pollen), pregnancy or other pre-existing conditions. Always check with your guests before serving and refer to the Thompson and Morgan list of edible flowers at **thompson-morgan.com/edible-flowers** for more detailed safety information.

Sourcing flowers

It is important not to use commercially grown flowers from florists and supermarkets. These are sprayed with non-edible chemicals and pesticides to keep them in good condition. Washing them doesn't get rid of these chemicals. They also tend to be stored in buckets of water not suitable for human consumption. My advice is to grow your own – or bribe neighbours, friends and family members who have gardens with the promise of cake in exchange for flowers. If you must buy them, source locally from gardens and florists who grow organically, or order from edible flower growers and farm shops.

Decorating with edible flowers

You can create beautiful, show-stopping cakes with whole flowers or a sprinkle of petals. Think about colour combinations, shape, size and form.

A few things to consider:

• **There is only a short window for working with fresh edible flowers.** Place on your cakes as soon as possible to avoid wilting. Flowers last for 3–4 hours on the cake.

• **If growing your own or sourcing from a garden,** pick the flowers on a dry day, early in the morning. Spread on a tray for 5 minutes – this allows any insects in the flowers to escape.

• **Store the flowers in the fridge** in a container with a loose lid, lined with paper towel for 3–4 days.

• **When decorating,** press delicate flowers onto the buttercream; more sturdy ones like rose and dahlias can be just placed on the cake.

• **If you need to secure the flowers,** do this at angles, using flowers with small stems still attached (check the stems are edible first). Dip the stems in melted chocolate and let them set before inserting into the cake, if you like. Secure heavier flowers with cocktail sticks – just be sure to mention this when serving the cake!

• **Discard the flowers before eating** – most are tasteless, used to add beauty.

Drying flowers

Seasonal edible flowers can be dried for use through the year. Flower-pressing kits are inexpensive, come in various sizes and last a long time. Pressed and dried flowers can be stored in a storage box, lined with paper towels, for a few months.

You can also use the old-fashioned method of placing flowers between pages of a book and weighing them down for a couple of weeks, then storing as above.

Some flowers like marigolds, calendula, cornflowers and roses can be dried by just leaving them outside: pluck the petals and let them dry on baking paper for 2–3 days, then store as above. You can also find dried edible flowers online.

Floral syrups

Syrups capture the flavour of stronger-tasting flowers (opposite) to last all year. Make a simple syrup (page 46), then, while still warm, infuse it with flowers for 6–24 hours, depending on the desired intensity. Store for up to 2 weeks in the fridge.

Sugar-coated edible flowers

Another method for preserving decorative flowers is to coat them in caster sugar and egg white. This is time-consuming but rewarding. Set aside a few hours, make space on a table and take a seat to do this.

1 Line a tray with a sheet of baking paper.

2 Put the sugar in a large bowl.

3 Put the egg white in a small bowl and gently whisk in 1 teaspoon of water using a fork for under a minute. Now take a small, perfectly clean brush, select a flower petal or flower and brush it all over with egg white.

4 Using a teaspoon, sprinkle it with sugar, covering it completely. Place the coated flower on the baking paper to dry.

5 Repeat this for all the flowers and petals. Leave them to dry for 10–12 hours and they will firm up and be ready to use. You can store them in an airtight container for a few weeks, keeping them separate with sheets of paper.

· 200g (generous 1 cup) white caster sugar
· 1 egg white
· edible flowers or petals

Common edible flowers (petals only) and leaves

Flowers

alliums
alyssum
anchusa
antirrhinum
begonia
  (tuberosa
  only)
Bellis daisy
calendula
carnation
chamomile
citrus flowers
clover
cornflower
dahlia
dandelion

daylily
dianthus
elderflower
evening
  primrose
fennel
forget-me-not
gladiolus
hibiscus
hollyhock
jasmine
lavender
lilac
magnolia
mallow
mimosa
nasturtium
pansy

phlox
  (perennial
  only)
pineapple
  sage
primrose
primula
rose
*rose scented
  geranium*
runner bean
  flowers (red
  only)
shungiku
stocks
strawberry
sunflower
sweet violet

tagetes
violet
viola
zinnia

Leaves

alyssum
angelica
basil
clover
fennel
lemon balm
*lemon
  verbena*
nasturtium
sweet cicely

Key:
common
allergen
dries well
stronger-
tasting

Storing cake

There is nothing like a freshly baked cake, but if you need to store your cake, follow these tips:

· **Sponge cakes made with butter quickly become stale and dry.** These are best enjoyed freshly baked.

· **I rarely store cakes in the fridge: they dry out faster and develop a stale 'fridge taste'.** As long as the cake is not filled with fresh cream, curd, fruits and berries, it can be stored, wrapped well in an airtight container or under a glass dome on the kitchen counter for 2 days. You can store plain cakes in this way, ready to be used in layer cakes – just add the fillings and decoration later.

· **Layered sponge cakes filled with fresh cream and topped with fresh fruits need to be stored in the fridge and eaten within a day or two.** These cakes don't freeze well, in my experience.

· **If you do need to store sponge cakes for longer, freeze them instead – before fillings have been added.** Wrap well in cling film (plastic wrap) and then store in freezer-friendly boxes or bags. Plain sponge cakes can be stored this way for a month or two. Store whole and defrost when needed, then cut, add fillings and decorate. They can also be cut in portions and frozen, well-wrapped, ready to be defrosted for cake emergencies.

· **To defrost frozen plain cakes,** place them still wrapped on the counter for a few hours then use as required, removing any wrapping once fully thawed.

· **Full buttercream cakes can be frozen for a week or two,** if you want to plan ahead for events and celebrations. To do this, make the buttercream cake up to the final buttercream layer (see page 34) and place the cake in the freezer for 3–4 hours to chill completely. Once frozen, take it out and wrap neatly with 2 or 3 layers of cling film. As it is frozen it is easier to wrap without messing up the buttercream finish. Once wrapped, place the cake back in the freezer for a week or two.

· **To defrost buttercream cakes,** it's important to remove the cling film while the cake is still frozen. Then place the cake in the fridge to defrost to avoid any cracks developing due to temperature fluctuation.

· **Freeze simple everyday cakes with fruits and berries in the batter for up to a month** wrapped and stored in suitable containers, although the texture of the fruits will change.

· **Cakes made with lots of dried fruits, nut powders and oil tend to have a longer shelf life.** Wrapped well and stored in airtight containers, they last for days, sometimes even weeks.

Transporting cake

If your friends and family know you love to bake, chances are you will be baking regularly for get-togethers and celebrations. Suddenly, baking becomes the easy bit and transporting the cake safely is the concern.

Here are my tried and tested tips:

· **If you need to travel, plan ahead and choose a cake where weather, temperature and travel time won't be a concern.** Then finish with berries, cream and flowers once you arrive.

· **If you often travel with cake, invest in a plastic cake caddy with a clip-on lid and a carry handle.** Alternatively, sturdy cake boxes made of paper or card can be bought online and in good cake or cook shops. I use a 25cm (10in) box with sides 15cm (6in) high for the 20cm (8in) cakes in this book.

· **Cake cards and cake drums provide a solid base when travelling.** The cakes should sit on cake boards bigger than the cake: a 20cm (8in) single-layer cake will sit on a 25cm (10in) cake drum or sturdy, thick cake card, inside a 25cm (10in) square cake box. That way, the cake board fits snugly in the box and there is no movement when travelling.

· **When travelling by car, the boot (trunk) is where I place my boxes.** Make sure anything else in the boot is secure and won't hit the cake. Anti-slip mats, available online and in car accessory shops, come in a roll and can be cut as needed. I cut a large piece and place in an empty boot, then put my cake box on top. Like magic, it doesn't move. I have travelled with wedding cakes this way for long distances. Drive carefully and avoid harsh braking, but this works.

· **For buttercream cakes, I ONLY use Swiss meringue buttercream as it is the most stable.** Once you layer and buttercream your cake, you need to freeze it well – at least 3-4 hours, or longer if travelling long distances, the weather is hot or if you are setting up a wedding. Once well-chilled, pack the cakes in suitable boxes.

· **If you are travelling with a tall cake or tiered cake, dowelling the cake becomes very important.** Refer to page 35 for cake dowelling. This helps to keep the cake secure and prevents sliding.

· **Decorate the cake at your destination,** especially if working with fresh edible flowers.

Classic cakes revisited

I have baked many versions of these cakes over the years and always come back to the recipes listed here. I hope you will tweak them further and make these recipes your own – such is the joy of sharing recipes.

I love the simplicity and unfussiness of single-layer cakes, but if you want something more elaborate, these cakes can be sliced in half and layered with your choice of fillings to make sandwich cakes (see page 32).

These cakes (except the marmalade and ginger cakes) also work well as taller buttercream cakes: double the recipes, divide the batter between two or three 20cm (8in) round tins, then follow the instructions for assembly on page 34.

Coffee and walnut cake

I am a tea lover and it took me some time to warm to the idea of coffee and walnut cake. To my surprise, I really liked the bitterness of the coffee with the crunch of the walnuts. My version includes lightly toasted walnuts, for a more satisfying nutty crunch, and a coffee caramel glaze.

1 Butter and flour a 20cm (8in) round cake tin. Line the base with a disc of baking paper. Preheat the oven to 170°C fan/190°C/375°F/Gas mark 5.

2 Spread the walnuts on a baking tray and roast for 5–7 minutes. Keep an eye on them as they can burn quickly. Allow to cool then chop coarsely, sprinkle with a tablespoonful of flour, mix and set aside.

3 Sift the flour, baking powder and salt into a bowl.

4 Mix the dissolved coffee and soured cream in a small jug.

5 Put the butter, both sugars and the vanilla in a large bowl, if using hand-held beaters, or a stand mixer with a beater attachment. Cream for 6–8 minutes until pale and fluffy. Add the eggs, one by one, incorporating well after each addition.

6 Add a third of the flour mixture followed by a third of the coffee and cream mixture, stirring after each addition. Continue to add alternately until everything is incorporated.

7 Set aside a handful of the chopped walnuts. Add the rest to the batter and gently mix in, then pour the batter into the prepared cake tin. Tap the tin gently on the worktop to release any air pockets.

8 Bake for 35–40 minutes, or until a skewer comes out clean and the cake is well-risen and springy to touch.

9 Cool the cake for 10 minutes in the tin, then invert onto a wire rack.

10 While the cake is cooling, make the glaze. Gently warm all the ingredients in a small pan until melted and homogeneous. Keep stirring over a gentle heat for 5 minutes until glossy and smooth. Remove from the heat and set aside but keep warm.

11 Brush the warm cake generously with a couple of coats of the glaze. Sprinkle with the reserved chopped walnuts and edible flowers, if you wish. Serve with whipped cream and any remaining caramel glaze.

- 180g (¾ cup plus 2 tsp) butter, plus extra for greasing
- 180g (1⅓ cups) self-raising (self-rising) flour, plus extra for dusting
- 150g (1½ cups) walnuts
- 1½ tsp baking powder
- ¼ tsp salt
- 4 Tbsp instant coffee powder dissolved in 2 Tbsp hot water
- 90ml (6 Tbsp) soured cream
- 100g (generous ½ cup) golden caster (superfine) sugar
- 100g (½ cup) light muscovado (light brown) sugar
- ½ tsp vanilla extract
- 4 eggs
- edible flowers, to decorate (optional)

For the glaze
- 100g (½ cup) light muscovado (light brown) sugar
- 100ml (7 Tbsp) double (heavy) cream
- 25g (scant 2 Tbsp) butter
- ½ tsp salt
- 2 Tbsp instant coffee powder

Marble cake

*Marble cake was the first cake I ever baked. In the late '80s, my aunt enrolled
in cooking classes. I still remember the red diary she wrote her recipes in.
Before she got married, we baked this cake together from that diary. I have
since made many versions of marble cakes and tweaked that original recipe
many times, but I have always kept the flavour close to the original. Maybe it's
the simplicity of it or the nostalgic flavour from my childhood, but this is the
cake I bake for myself. I have used brown butter as well as sunflower oil, which
keeps the cake soft and moist for a few days.*

1 Butter and flour a 20cm (8in) round cake tin, then line
the base with a disc of baking paper. Preheat the oven to
170°C fan/190°C/375°F/Gas mark 5.

2 Sift the flour, baking powder, bicarbonate of soda, salt and
custard powder into a large bowl.

3 Mix the melted brown butter and sunflower oil in a small jug.

4 Blend the cocoa and coffee with the milk in a small bowl.

5 Put the eggs, vanilla and both the sugars into the bowl of a
stand mixer with a whisk attachment or in a bowl if using a
hand-held whisk. Whisk for 5 minutes until pale and fluffy.

6 Now sift in the dry ingredients in three goes, folding in gently
to avoid deflating the whisked egg mixture. Gently pour in the
butter and oil from the side of the bowl. Fold it in. Stir gently.

7 Pour half the batter into another bowl. Keep one bowl of
batter vanilla. To the other, add the cocoa–coffee mix. Gently
fold it in. Both batters should have the same consistency: if one
is thicker, use a little milk to loosen it.

8 Put 2 tablespoons of the vanilla batter in the centre of the
prepared cake tin. Then add 2 tablespoons of the chocolate
batter in the centre of the vanilla batter. Repeat, adding
the batters alternately in the centre each time, creating a
concentric pattern, until both batters have been used up.

9 To create the marbled effect, take a toothpick or skewer and,
starting at the edge of the tin, push the skewer down into the
batter until it touches the base of the tin, then drag towards the
centre of the cake. Repeat to make 8 evenly spaced lines.

10 Tap the tin gently on the worktop to release any air pockets.
Bake for about 35 minutes, or until a skewer comes out clean.

11 Cool the cake for 10 minutes in the tin, then turn out onto a
wire rack. Allow to cool completely. If using, pour the chocolate
glaze over the cooled cake, then leave to set for an hour.

- butter, for greasing
- 185g (1 ⅓ cups) plain (all-purpose) flour,
  plus extra for dusting
- 1 tsp baking powder
- ½ tsp bicarbonate of soda (baking soda)
- ¼ tsp salt
- 25g (3 Tbsp) custard powder (instant
  vanilla pudding)
- 125g (½ cup plus 1 Tbsp) Brown Butter
  (page 46), from 160g (scant ¾ cup)
  butter, melted
- 90ml (6 Tbsp) sunflower oil
- 50g (about ½ cup) cocoa powder
- 1 Tbsp instant coffee powder
- 125ml (½ cup) milk
- 4 eggs
- 1 Tbsp vanilla bean paste or extract
- 125g (scant ¾ cup) golden caster
  (superfine) sugar
- 75g (⅓ cup plus 2 tsp) light brown
  soft sugar

To serve (optional)
- Chocolate Glaze (page 51)

Marmalade cake

This cake is for my parents. If it is Paddington Bear who loves marmalade the most, then my Papa comes a close second. He has a tiny teaspoonful after most meals, as he is not allowed to spread marmalade on his toast. I take a few jars with me when I visit their home. In addition, because my mum does not eat eggs, this recipe is egg-free.

The cake matures well and can be enjoyed days after it is made. It is good on the breakfast table too, if you have guests and want to bake ahead.

1 Butter and flour a 20cm (8in) round cake tin. Line the base and sides with baking paper. Preheat the oven to 170°C fan/190°C/375°F/Gas mark 5.

2 Put the mixed dried fruit and the orange juice in a small pan over a medium heat. Gently warm through for 5 minutes then set aside for the fruit to cool and absorb all the juice.

3 Put the oil, buttermilk, vanilla and 3 tablespoons of the marmalade in a small jug. Stir to mix.

4 Sift the flour, baking powder, bicarbonate of soda, salt and spice into a large mixing bowl. Add the soft dark brown sugar and orange zest, and mix well. Next, add the butter and rub the flour and butter well using your hands until the mixture resembles coarse sand.

5 Add in the soaked fruit and any remaining juice.

6 Slowly pour in the oil and buttermilk mix and stir until just combined. Do not overmix.

7 Pour the batter into the prepared tin. Tap the tin gently on the worktop to release any air pockets. Dot the 4 teaspoons of marmalade on top of the cake and gently swirl using a skewer. Sprinkle with the demerara sugar.

8 Bake for 45–50 minutes, checking after 40 minutes, or until a skewer comes out clean. It will be springy to touch, with a golden crust. Once out of the oven, it may sink in the middle slightly. Embrace this – it's delicious.

9 Cool the cake for 10 minutes in the tin, then turn out onto a wire rack and leave to cool completely. Brush the warm glaze over the top and sides of the cake and leave to set. Decorate with some candied orange slices and edible flower petals, if you like.

- 120g (generous ½ cup) butter, plus extra for greasing
- 250g (1¾ cups plus 2 Tbsp) plain (all-purpose) flour, plus extra for dusting
- 150g (5½oz) mixed dried fruit (chopped apricots, cranberries, candied mixed peel)
- zest and juice of 2 oranges
- 50ml (generous 3 Tbsp) sunflower oil
- 150ml (scant ⅔ cup) buttermilk
- ½ tsp vanilla extract
- 3 Tbsp plus 4 tsp Seville orange marmalade
- 3 tsp baking powder
- ½ tsp bicarbonate of soda (baking soda)
- ¼ tsp salt
- 2 tsp mixed spice
- 120g (⅔ cup minus 1 Tbsp) soft dark brown sugar
- 2 Tbsp demerara (raw brown) sugar

For the glaze
- 3 Tbsp Seville orange marmalade thinned with 2 Tbsp hot water

To decorate (optional)
- candied orange slices and edible flower petals

Carrot and pistachio cake

I wanted my carrot cake to mimic the decadence of halwa, a sweet Indian pudding – fragrant with spices, slow-cooked in milk and topped with nuts, with a fudge-like texture. I used to sell this cake at a market stall, and an impeccably dressed elderly couple – Maureen and John – would regularly ask for it. One day, they asked me to make their daughter's wedding cake – and so began my wedding-cake-making journey. Every time I make this cake I think of them. Thank you, Maureen and John.

1 Butter and flour a 20cm (8in) round cake tin. Line the base with a disc of baking paper. Preheat the oven to 170°C fan/190°C/375°F/Gas mark 5.

2 Sift the flours, baking powder, bicarbonate of soda, salt and nutmeg into a bowl. Grate the carrots using the fine side of a box grater.

3 Put the melted butter, sunflower oil, sugar, orange zest and juice, vanilla and 3 of the eggs into a large bowl. Using a balloon whisk, beat the mixture until well combined. Add the sifted flour mix, the carrots and pistachios, and give a few stirs until everything is just combined. Do not overmix.

4 Pour the batter into the prepared cake tin. Tap the tin gently on the worktop to release any air pockets.

5 Put the remaining egg in a separate bowl and add the cream cheese and pistachio paste, if using. Mix well. Dollop the cream cheese mixture on top of the cake batter then, using a long skewer, give it a few swirls.

6 Bake for 35–40 minutes, or until the surface is springy to touch and a skewer comes out clean.

7 Cool the cake for 10 minutes in the tin, then turn out onto a wire rack. Meanwhile, make the topping. Add all the ingredients, except the pistachio paste, to a large bowl. Whisk until just combined. Add the paste and mix until smooth and even.

8 Once the cake has completely cooled, place on a suitable serving plate or cake board.

9 Spread with the topping and sprinkle with pistachio nibs. Decorate with some edible flowers, if you like.

10 This cake is best eaten on the day it is made.

- 75g (5 Tbsp) butter, melted, plus extra for greasing
- 100g (¾ cup) plain (all-purpose) flour, plus extra for dusting
- 100g (¾ cup) wholemeal (wholewheat) flour
- 1 tsp baking powder
- ½ tsp bicarbonate of soda (baking soda)
- ½ tsp salt
- ¼ tsp freshly grated nutmeg
- 300g (10½oz) carrots, peeled
- 100ml (7 Tbsp) sunflower oil
- 150g (¾ cup) light muscovado (light brown) sugar
- zest and juice of 1 large orange
- 1 tsp vanilla extract
- 4 eggs
- 100g (about 1 cup) finely chopped pistachios
- 125g (generous ½ cup) cream cheese
- 50g (5 Tbsp) pistachio paste (optional)

For the topping
- 150g (scant ¾ cup) cream cheese, at room temperature
- 100ml (7 Tbsp) double (heavy) cream
- 1 tsp vanilla extract
- 25g (2¾ Tbsp) icing (confectioners') sugar
- 50g (5 Tbsp) pistachio paste

To decorate
- 50g (about ½ cup) pistachio nibs or chopped pistachios
- edible flowers (optional)

Spiced ginger cake

I love ginger in all its forms. It finds its way into my morning tea and into my everyday cooking too. Before I tasted a ginger cake on holiday, I hadn't realized how varied ginger bakes could be: Yorkshire parkin; Jamaican ginger cake; Grasmere gingerbread; Christmas gingerbread. When the weather starts getting cold, make this flavourful and warming cake – spiced with clove, nutmeg and all four forms of ginger – on repeat and enjoy with lots of tea. It matures with keeping and is delicious after a day or two. It will keep for a week in an airtight container.

1 Butter and flour a 20cm (8in) round cake tin. Line the base with a disc of baking paper. Preheat the oven to 160°C fan/180°C/350°F/Gas mark 4.

2 Put the butter, sugar, grated ginger, treacle and syrup in a medium pan over a gentle heat. Leave to melt, then stir until everything is homogeneous and smooth. Turn off the heat and set this wet mix aside.

3 Sift the flour, baking powder, bicarbonate of soda, ground ginger, cloves, nutmeg, cinnamon and salt into a large bowl. Make a well in the centre. Set this dry mix aside.

4 Put the eggs, milk and vanilla in a small jug and stir together.

5 Pour the wet mix into the dry mix. Give it a good stir with a spatula to combine. Pour in the egg mixture and stir again until just combined. Chop the stem ginger and mix it into the batter.

6 Pour the batter into the prepared tin and tap the tin gently on the worktop to release any air pockets. Bake for 40–45 minutes. After 30 minutes cover with foil if it is browning too much. The cake is ready when the surface is springy to touch and a skewer comes out clean.

7 Cool the cake for 10 minutes in the tin, then turn out onto a wire rack. Mix the syrup from the stem ginger jar with 2 tablespoons of boiling water and brush it all over the cake. Leave to soak in as the cake cools.

8 If you are decorating your cake, once it is completely cold, mix the icing sugar, ground ginger and salt with 3–4 tablespoons of cold water to make an icing glaze of pouring consistency. Pour over the cake, covering the top and sides, using the back of a spoon or silicone brush to help. While this is still wet, scatter with the crystallized ginger and edible flowers. Leave to set completely for a couple of hours.

- 200g (¾ cup plus 2 Tbsp) butter, plus extra for greasing
- 350g (2 ⅔ cups) plain (all-purpose) flour, plus extra for dusting
- 140g (¾ cup) dark soft brown sugar
- 5cm (2in) knob of fresh ginger root, peeled and grated
- 50ml (about 3 Tbsp) black treacle (optional)
- 100ml (7 Tbsp) golden (dark corn) syrup
- 2 tsp baking powder
- ½ tsp bicarbonate of soda (baking soda)
- 2 tsp ground ginger
- ½ tsp ground cloves
- 1 tsp freshly grated nutmeg
- ½ tsp ground cinnamon
- ½ tsp salt
- 3 eggs
- 125ml (½ cup) milk
- 1 tsp vanilla extract
- 8 balls of stem ginger and 6 Tbsp syrup from the jar

To decorate (optional)

- 150g (about 1 cup) unsifted icing (confectioners') sugar
- ¼ tsp ground ginger
- ¼ tsp salt
- 10g (¼oz) crystallized (candied) ginger, chopped
- edible flowers

Chocolate fudge cake

I am not a chocolate person, but my husband is. After a lot of trials, this recipe is now my go-to single-layer chocolate cake (see page 213 for the buttercream version). I have used it for many birthday celebrations and wedding cakes, both for family members and for orders. It is very simple to make – no gadgets or special equipment needed, just a few bowls and a spatula.

1 First make the ganache, following the method on page 51.

2 Butter and dust with cocoa powder a 20cm (8in) round cake tin. Line the base with a disc of baking paper. Preheat the oven to 170°C fan/190°C/375°F/Gas mark 5.

3 Melt the butter and both chocolates in a glass or metal bowl over a pan of barely simmering water.

4 Sift the flour, baking powder, bicarbonate of soda, salt and cocoa powder into a large bowl. Then add both the sugars and sift again.

5 Mix the eggs, buttermilk and vanilla in a small jug.

6 Pour the hot butter–chocolate mixture and hot coffee into the dry ingredients and fold in with a spatula. Then add in the egg and buttermilk mixture. Gently fold in until it all comes together. Pour the batter into the tin and give the tin a gentle tap on the counter to release any air pockets.

7 Bake for 35–40 minutes, or until a skewer comes out with a few crumbs clinging to it; I find chocolate cakes are better slightly underbaked than overbaked.

8 Cool the cake for 10 minutes in the tin, then turn out onto a wire rack. Allow to cool completely, then spoon the chocolate ganache over the top of the cake and swirl using the back of a spoon. Let it cool and set.

9 Decorate with a few edible flowers and spray with some gold dust, if you wish.

- 135g (½ cup plus 1½ Tbsp) butter, plus extra for greasing
- 50g (½ cup) cocoa powder, plus extra for dusting
- 75g (2½oz) 70% dark (bittersweet) chocolate, broken into pieces
- 75g (2½oz) milk chocolate, broken into pieces
- 125g (1 cup minus 1 Tbsp) plain (all-purpose) flour
- 1 tsp baking powder
- ½ tsp bicarbonate of soda (baking soda)
- ¼ tsp salt
- 75g (generous ⅓ cup) golden caster (superfine) sugar
- 100g (½ cup) light muscovado sugar
- 3 large eggs
- 75ml (5 Tbsp) buttermilk
- 1 tsp vanilla extract
- 1 Tbsp instant coffee dissolved in 75ml (5 Tbsp) boiling water
- 1 batch of Chocolate Ganache (page 51)

To decorate (optional)
- edible flowers
- gold dust

Victoria sponge cake

A Victoria sponge is easy to put together and is probably one of the first cakes that anyone bakes, but its simplicity means there is nowhere to hide. You want to use the best eggs, butter, vanilla, cream and in-season strawberries. No summer table should be without a Victoria sponge.

---

1 Butter and flour a 20cm (8in) round cake tin. Line the base with a disc of baking paper. Preheat the oven to 170°C fan/190°C/375°F/Gas mark 5.

2 Sift the flour, baking powder and salt into a large bowl.

3 Break the eggs into a small jug and stir until they are just mixed.

4 Put the brown butter, sugar and vanilla into the bowl of a stand mixer with the beater attachment (or use hand-held beaters and a large bowl). Cream until the mixture is pale and fluffy. Gradually add the eggs in 3–4 goes, beating well after each addition.

5 Sift in the flour mixture in 3–4 goes, gently folding it in. Add the soured cream and fold it in gently. Do not overmix the batter.

6 Spoon the cake batter into the prepared tin. Tap the tin gently on the worktop to release any air pockets.

7 Bake for 35–40 minutes. After 30 minutes cover with foil if it is browning too much. The cake is ready when the surface is springy to touch and a skewer comes out clean.

8 Cool the cake for 10 minutes in the tin, then turn out onto a wire rack.

9 Meanwhile, wash the strawberries and remove the stalks. Slice into quarters and sprinkle with sugar. Macerate for 10 minutes.

10 Whip the cream with the icing sugar and vanilla until soft peaks form. Spoon the cream over the cooled cake. Dollop spoonfuls of the strawberry jam and the strawberries on top. Decorate with some edible flowers, if you like.

11 Now cut a large slice and find a quiet corner in which to indulge!

- butter, for greasing
- 200g (1½ cups) plain (all-purpose) flour, plus extra for dusting
- 1½ tsp baking powder
- ¼ tsp sea salt
- 4 eggs
- 175g (¾ cup plus 1 tsp) Brown Butter (page 46), from 220g (1 cup) butter
- 175g (1 cup) golden caster (superfine) sugar
- 1 tsp vanilla bean paste
- 50ml (3 Tbsp) soured cream

For the topping
- 150g (5½oz) fresh strawberries
- 25g (2¾ Tbsp) golden caster (superfine) sugar
- 250ml (1 cup) double (heavy) cream
- 25g (2¾ Tbsp) icing (confectioners') sugar
- 1 tsp vanilla bean paste
- 5 Tbsp strawberry jam (jelly)
- edible flowers (optional)

Lemon drizzle cake

Before I moved to the UK, my love for lemons was limited to savoury dishes, lemonade and shikanji, an Indian lemon drink. It wasn't until 2001 – on the third day of my new life in the UK – that I tried lemon cake. I didn't know then that it would become my favourite.

When Amit and I were staying with my in-laws in Wales, I ordered my first ever lemon cake in a café overlooking Harlech Castle. Amit and I were married only the week before so my hands were still covered with the elaborate wedding henna design. Our waitress was intrigued, and we spoke about India, cakes and the sea. I think she was the first person outside the Indian friend-and-family diaspora I spoke to. That cake was a revelation to me. I now bake some version of a lemon cake almost every week and even grow lemons in my little London garden.

---

1 Butter and flour a 20cm (8in) round cake tin and line the base and sides with baking paper. Preheat the oven to 170°C fan/190°C/375°F/Gas mark 5.

2 Stir together the melted butter, cream, vanilla and lemon juice in a small jug.

3 Sift the flour, baking powder and salt into a bowl.

4 Put the lemon zest and caster sugar into a large bowl if using a hand-held whisk, or a stand mixer with a whisk attachment. Rub together using your hands to infuse the sugar with the lemon flavour.

5 Add the eggs to the lemon-infused sugar and whisk for 4–5 minutes until pale, fluffy and doubled in volume. Slowly pour the melted butter and cream mix into the whisked egg mixture. Gently fold using a large metal spoon or spatula in 3–4 goes. Now add the sifted flour in 2–3 goes. Fold in gently, taking care not to deflate the batter.

6 Pour the batter into the prepared tin and tap the tin gently on the counter to release any air pockets.

7 Bake for 40 minutes, or until the surface is springy to touch and a skewer comes out clean. Remove the cake from the oven and reduce the temperature to 150°C fan/170°C/340°F/Gas mark 3½.

Continued...

- 100g (½ cup minus 1 Tbsp) butter, melted, plus extra for greasing
- 250g (1¾ cups plus 2 Tbsp) plain (all-purpose) flour, plus extra for dusting
- 150ml (⅔ cup) double (heavy) cream
- 1 tsp vanilla extract
- 3 Tbsp lemon juice
- 1½ tsp baking powder
- ¼ tsp salt
- zest of 4 lemons
- 300g (scant 1¾ cups) golden caster (superfine) sugar
- 5 eggs
- edible flowers, to decorate

For the glaze (optional)
- 4 Tbsp apricot jam (jelly), sieved and thinned with 2 Tbsp hot water

For the drizzle
- 250g (1½ cups minus 1 Tbsp) icing (confectioners') sugar
- juice of 1 lemon
- pinch of salt

8 Cool the cake for 10 minutes in the tin, then gently turn it out onto a wire rack set over a baking tray. If using the glaze, brush the cake all over with the thinned apricot jam and let it set for another 10 minutes.

9 Meanwhile, make the drizzle by mix the icing sugar, lemon juice and salt to make an icing glaze of pouring consistency.

10 Once the apricot glaze is dry to touch, cover the entire cake with the drizzle. Return the cake (still over the baking tray) to the oven for 3 minutes for the drizzle to set. Do keep an eye on the clock and don't walk away. Timing is important here.

11 After 3 minutes, take the cake out of the oven and let it cool on the rack completely. Sprinkle with edible flowers to decorate.

Note:

The apricot glaze is optional but recommended: it helps to lock in the moisture and keep the cake fresh for 3–4 days. Placing the cake back in the oven sets the drizzle to a translucent glaze.

Pineapple upside-down cake

This is the grown-up version of pineapple upside-down cake, using the classic store-cupboard ingredients of canned pineapple and glacé cherries, but with the freshness of lime zest and chilli-glazed pineapple slices – though you can leave out the chilli if it's not to your taste.

1 Butter and flour a 20cm (8in) round cake tin. Line the base with a disc of baking paper. Preheat the oven to 170°C fan/190°C/375°F/Gas mark 5.

2 First make the sugar-butter layer. In a small bowl, mix together the sugar and butter, using a fork or your hands, until just combined. Dollop evenly into the prepared tin.

3 Place the pineapple slices on paper towel and wipe them dry. Cut them into half-moon shapes and arrange them on top of the sugar-butter layer in the cake tin. (You may not need all of them but pack them as tightly as you can.) Set aside while you make the batter.

4 Sift the flour, baking powder and salt into a bowl.

5 Break the eggs into a small jug and gently stir with a fork until just mixed.

6 Put the butter, sugar and lime zest into a large bowl if using a hand-held beater, or a stand mixer with a beater attachment. Cream until pale and fluffy. This should take about 5–8 minutes on medium speed. Gradually add the eggs in 3–4 goes, beating well after each addition. Add the flour mix in 2–3 goes, followed by the vanilla. Gently stir the batter, then lightly fold in the soured cream and lime juice.

7 Spoon the batter over the arranged pineapple slices in the tin. Level the batter and give the tin a gentle tap on the counter to remove any air pockets. Bake for about 45 minutes until the cake has risen, the surface is golden and a skewer comes out clean.

Continued...

- 225g (1 cup plus 2 Tbsp) butter, plus extra for greasing
- 225g (1¾ cups) plain (all-purpose) flour, plus extra to dust
- 8 canned pineapple rings in juice (about 435g/15½oz)
- 2 tsp baking powder
- ½ tsp salt
- 4 eggs
- 225g (1½ cups) golden caster (superfine) sugar
- zest and juice of 1 lime
- 1 tsp vanilla bean paste
- 75ml (¼ cup plus 1 Tbsp) soured cream

For the sugar-butter layer
- 100g (generous ½ cup) golden caster (superfine) sugar
- 75g (3½ Tbsp) butter

Glazed pineapple (optional)
- 50g (3½ Tbsp) butter
- 50g (generous ¼ cup) golden caster (superfine) sugar
- 8 canned pineapple rings in juice (about 435g/15½oz)
- 1 fresh long red chilli, seeds removed, very finely chopped
- zest of 1 lime
- 1 tsp vanilla bean paste

8 Once the cake is baked, let it rest for 5 minutes exactly. Then carefully invert onto a cake serving plate. If any of the pineapple slices have moved, reposition them. The cake is ready to eat at this stage, eaten hot or cold. I like it warm with glazed chilli and lime pineapple as suggested below.

9 To make the glazed pineapple, put the butter in a medium frying pan (skillet) over a low heat. Sprinkle in half the sugar. Cut the pineapple rings cut in half and place in the pan in a single layer. Sprinkle in the remaining sugar, chopped red chilli, lime zest and vanilla bean paste. Increase the heat to medium and allow the pineapple to caramelize slightly on one side then turn the slices over to caramelize the other side. Turn off the heat and arrange the slices over the cake, spooning with extra juices from the pan. Serve warm with lots of clotted cream or vanilla ice cream.

Old-fashioned cherry or tutti-frutti cake

*Growing up in India in the 1980s and '90s, cherry, or 'tutti-frutti',
cake, as it was fondly called, was everywhere – at corner shops, railway
stations, roadside tea stalls and in school, university and office canteens.
It was studded with tutti-frutti flecks or red cherries (though I am not sure
they were real cherries back then) and was quite dry, almost like bread.
It is still available in all the places I mention here.*

*Years later, I tasted an old-fashioned cherry cake at a National Trust café
in Devon. It instantly tasted familiar, only better – buttery and moist, and
this time with real glacé cherries. That weekend, I baked a cherry cake.
Over the years I have tweaked it to this version here. Make it for your
parents and grandparents or an elderly neighbour and see them smile
– or introduce it to the next generation. We need to bring this classic back.*

---

1 Butter and flour a 20cm (8in) round cake tin. Line the
sides and base with baking paper. Preheat the oven to
170°C fan/190°C/375°F/Gas mark 5.

2 Drain off any syrup from the cherries using a large sieve
(strainer) and give them a quick rinse. Pat them dry on paper
towel and cut them in half.

3 Put the cherries in a bowl with the dried apricots, angelica
and tutti-frutti mix, if using. Dust with a tablespoon of flour,
stir and set aside.

4 Sift the flour, custard powder, baking powder, salt and
ground almonds into a large bowl.

5 Break the eggs into a small jug and stir with a fork until they
are just mixed.

6 Put the butter, oil, sugar, almond extract and vanilla into a
stand mixer, or large bowl if using hand-held beaters. Cream
until the mixture is pale and fluffy. Gradually add the eggs in
3–4 goes, beating well after each addition.

7 Sift in the flour mix in 3–4 goes, gently folding it in using
a large metal spoon or spatula. Do not overmix. Add half the
cherry/dried fruit mix and finally the soured cream. Give it
one last stir.

Continued…

- 200g (¾ cup plus 2 Tbsp) butter,
  plus extra for greasing
- 225g (about 1¾ cups) plain (all-purpose)
  flour, plus extra for dusting
- 200g (about 1½ cups) glacé cherries
- 100g (about ¾ cup) dried apricots,
  chopped
- 70g (about ½ cup) candied angelica,
  chopped (optional)
- 70g (about ½ cup) tutti-frutti mix
  (optional)
- 25g (3 Tbsp) custard powder
  (instant vanilla pudding)
- 1 tsp baking powder
- ¼ tsp salt
- 100g (about 1 cup) ground almonds
- 4 eggs
- 25ml (2½ Tbsp) sunflower oil
- 225g (1 cup plus 2 Tbsp) golden
  caster (superfine) sugar
- ¼ tsp almond extract (less is more here)
- 1 tsp vanilla bean paste
- 100ml (7 Tbsp) soured cream

To serve
- 60g (4 Tbsp) golden caster (superfine)
  sugar, for sprinkling
- edible flowers, to decorate (optional)

8 Spoon half the cake batter into the prepared tin, then spread the rest of the cherry/dried fruit mix on top. Spoon in the rest of the batter. Level the surface with the back of a spoon and push in any fruit to avoid it burning. Sprinkle the golden caster sugar, if using, evenly over the batter.

9 Bake for 45–50 minutes. After 30 minutes, cover with foil if it is browning too much. The cake is ready when the surface is springy to touch, a skewer comes out clean and there is a golden caster sugar crust on top. Don't worry if there are a few cracks.

10 Cool the cake for 10 minutes in the tin, then turn out onto a wire rack.

11 Decorate with edible flower petals if serving at a gathering – or just because you feel like it.

Fruit cake

My first taste of a fruit cake was a traditional, rich fruit cake at my own wedding, over 20 years ago. I really did not like it! I stayed away from similar fruit cakes for many years afterwards. Then, on my first trip to Scotland, I bought a small packaged cake topped with whole almonds, thinking it was an almond cake. When I cut into it, I found that it was a light fruit cake, and to my surprise I really enjoyed that version. I have tried many recipes since, but this is the one I make every Christmas.

1 The night before you want to bake, chop all the dried fruits (except the cranberries) and mixed peel, if not already chopped, then soak in the whisky or tea and orange juice. Leave, covered, overnight or for at least 6 hours at room temperature.

2 Butter and double-line with baking paper the base and sides of a 20cm (8in) round cake tin. Preheat the oven to 160°C fan/180°C/350°F/Gas mark 4.

3 Sift the flour, baking powder, almonds, spices and salt into a bowl.

4 Put the butter and sugar in a large bowl if using hand-held beaters, or a stand mixer with a beater attachment. Cream until pale and fluffy. Add the eggs one by one, beating well between each addition. Sift in the flour and spice mix in 3–4 goes. Add the soaked fruit, cranberries and grated apple and zest. Give everything a good gentle stir.

5 Spoon the batter into the prepared tin. Level it with the back of a spoon and give the tin a gentle tap on the counter to release any air pockets.

6 Bake for 50–60 minutes, or until a skewer comes out clean. After 30 minutes, cover with foil if it is browning too much.

7 Cool the cake for 15 minutes in the tin, then turn out onto a wire rack. Leave to cool completely.

8 To decorate, roll out the marzipan to form a 20cm (8in) disc. Brush the surface of the cooled cake with apricot jam, then place the marzipan disc on top. Crimp the edges if you wish. Brush the marzipan with the saffron water, if using. Finish with whole almonds and candied fruits.

9 Well-wrapped and stored in an airtight tin, the cake will last for up to 2 weeks.

- 200g (¾ cup plus 2 Tbsp) butter, plus extra for greasing
- 100g (about ⅔ cup) soft dried figs
- 75g (about ½ cup) soft dried apricots
- 75g (about ½ cup) good-quality glacé cherries
- 75g (about ½ cup) dried mango (optional)
- 50g (scant ½ cup) dried cranberries
- 150g (generous 1 cup) good-quality mixed citrus peel
- 100ml (7 Tbsp) good-quality whisky or freshly brewed tea
- zest and juice of 2 oranges
- 200g (1½ cups) plain (all-purpose) flour
- 1 tsp baking powder
- 50g (½ cup) ground almonds
- 1 tsp ground cinnamon
- 1 tsp mixed spice
- 1 tsp ground ginger
- ¼ whole nutmeg, freshly grated
- ¼ tsp salt
- 200g (1 cup) light muscovado sugar
- 3 large eggs
- 1 eating apple, cored and grated (no need to peel)

To decorate (optional)
- 300g (10½oz) good-quality marzipan
- 2 Tbsp apricot jam (jelly), sieved
- ¼ tsp saffron strands soaked in 1 Tbsp hot water (optional)
- 50g (about ⅓ cup) blanched whole almonds, lightly toasted
- whole candied fruits, such as figs, pears, cherries, small oranges or orange rings, etc.

Seasonal everyday cakes

This chapter is for those times when you need a simple cake – one that can be enjoyed warm out of the oven either with tea or as a dessert, and that is equally delicious three days later.

These recipes celebrate the seasons and make the most of the abundance of fruits and berries through the year.

Some ingredients may seem elaborate but the process is simple, and this is a good time to experiment with flavour based on what's in season and what you like best. They are easy to put together and, once baked, are delicious warm or cold.

Passion fruit, cardamom and olive oil cake

I love the fragrance, freshness and sharpness of passion fruit. The fresh fruit varies in size and ripeness so purée (available online) often works better in cake. Freeze leftover purée for cocktails or to flavour ice creams.

This recipe is good with melted butter or oil. In fact, I used to make it with butter, but once used an extra virgin olive oil out of necessity. Its mild, warm herbal notes worked so well that I now always use oil.

1 Brush a 20cm (8in) round cake tin with oil or butter and dust with flour. Line the base and sides with baking paper. Preheat the oven to 160°C fan/180°C/350°F/Gas mark 4.

2 Sift the flour, salt, baking powder, turmeric, almonds and ground pistachios into a bowl.

3 In a large jug, mix together the olive oil or melted butter, passion fruit purée, soured cream and vanilla.

4 Put the eggs, sugar and lemon zest in a large bowl, if using a hand-held whisk, or a stand mixer with a whisk attachment. Whisk for 6–8 minutes until the batter is pale, has tripled in volume and the whisk leaves a ribbon trail.

5 Add the sifted dry ingredients to the egg mixture in 3–4 goes, gently folding in after each addition with a large metal spoon. Take care not to deflate the batter.

6 Slowly drizzle the oil and passion fruit purée mixture into the batter and gently fold in. Make sure the batter is mixed properly and there is no liquid in the base of the bowl.

7 Pour the batter into the prepared tin. Gently tap the tin a couple of times on the counter to release any air pockets. Bake on the middle shelf of the oven for 45 minutes, or until a skewer comes out clean.

8 Meanwhile, make the syrup. Put the ingredients in a small pan over a medium heat. Allow the sugar to dissolve, then simmer for 5–7 minutes. Turn off the heat and set aside.

Continued...

- 200ml (¾ cup plus 1 Tbsp) extra virgin olive oil or 200g (¾ cup plus 2 Tbsp) butter, melted, plus extra for greasing
- 250g (1¾ cups plus 2 Tbsp) self-raising (self-rising) flour, plus extra for dusting
- ¼ tsp sea salt
- 1 tsp baking powder
- ¼ tsp ground turmeric (optional, but it adds great colour)
- 75g (about ¾ cup) ground almonds
- 100g (1 cup) ground pistachios (see page 19)
- 75ml (5 Tbsp) passion fruit purée
- 100ml (7 Tbsp) soured cream
- 1 Tbsp vanilla extract
- 5 large eggs
- 300g (scant 1¾ cups) golden caster (superfine) sugar
- zest of 2 lemons, juice saved for the syrup

For the passion fruit syrup
- 100ml (7 Tbsp) passion fruit purée
- 125g (⅔ cup) golden caster (superfine) sugar
- juice of 2 lemons
- ¼ tsp sea salt

For the ganache drizzle (optional)
- 100g (3 ½ oz) white chocolate, finely chopped
- 150ml (½ cup plus 1 Tbsp) double (heavy) cream
- 50ml (about 3 Tbsp) passion fruit purée
- 30g (1 Tbsp) pistachio nibs or finely chopped nuts, plus extra to decorate

9 Once the cake is cooked, leave it in the tin for 10 minutes, then turn out onto a wire rack to cool slightly. Brush the syrup over the top and sides of the cake. Give it 2–3 coats for a lovely sheen, then leave the syrup to soak in and the cake to cool completely.

10 If using the ganache drizzle, wait for the cake to cool completely. Put the chocolate in a medium bowl. Warm the cream in a small pan over a low heat. Bring to a gentle simmer, then turn off the heat and stir in the passion fruit purée. Pour this over the chopped chocolate. Leave for 5 minutes, then stir to a glossy, runny ganache. Add the chopped pistachios. Pour the ganache over the cake so that it is completely encased. Decorate with more pistachios, if you wish.

Apricot, rose and sesame cake

The rose flavour is very subtle here, just a hint in the background. You can leave it out if you don't like it, but it complements the apricots well. Supermarket apricots can lack sweetness: look for small ones in Middle Eastern stores or specialist fresh fruit grocers, when in season. A little sugar and heat helps to bring out their flavour. Sesame seeds add a delicious crust around the cake while tahini brings a nutty, warming note that I adore.

1 To make the compôte, put the apricots, cracked cardamom pods, sugar, lemon zest and juice and salt in a medium pan. Add the cornflour paste. Simmer gently over a low heat for about 12–15 minutes, or until the apricots are soft and jammy but holding their shape. Stir a couple of times to avoid burning. Once cooked, add the rose water. Leave to cool completely, then discard the cardamom pods.

Tip The compôte will last in the fridge for a few weeks and can easily be scaled up. It is delicious spread on toast or spooned over yoghurt and granola.

2 Preheat the oven to 170°C fan/190°C/375°F/Gas mark 5.

3 Generously butter a 20cm (8in) round cake tin. Sprinkle the 50g (¼ cup) of sesame seeds over the base to cover the buttered area in an even layer. This creates the crust so be generous with the butter and seeds. Chill the prepared tin in the fridge or freezer while you make the batter.

4 Sift the flour, baking powder, salt and ground cardamom into a large mixing bowl. Stir in the ground almonds, polenta and 200g (1 cup) sesame seeds.

5 Break the eggs into a small jug. Lightly whisk with a fork.

6 Put the butter, tahini, sugar, lemon zest, rose and vanilla extracts into a large bowl if using a hand-held beater, or a stand mixer, and beat until pale and fluffy, about 5–6 minutes.

Continued...

- 175g (¾ cup pus 1 tsp) butter, plus extra for greasing
- 200g (1 cup) sesame seeds, plus 50g (¼ cup) for the tin
- 175g (1 ⅓ cups) plain (all-purpose) flour
- 1½ tsp baking powder
- ¼ tsp salt
- ¼ tsp ground cardamom
- 100g (1 cup) ground almonds
- 75g (½ cup) fine polenta
- 4 eggs
- 75g (about 4 Tbsp) tahini
- 175g (1 cup) golden caster (superfine) sugar, plus 50g (¼ cup) to sprinkle
- zest of 1 lemon
- ½ tsp rose water (optional)
- ¼ tsp vanilla extract
- 250g (9oz) fresh apricots, halved and stoned

For the apricot compôte

- 250g (9oz) fresh apricots, stoned and roughly chopped
- 4–5 green cardamom pods, cracked but with the seeds intact
- 50g (¼ cup) caster (superfine) sugar
- zest and juice of 1 lemon
- ½ tsp sea salt
- 1 Tbsp cornflour (cornstarch) mixed with 50ml (3 Tbsp plus 1 tsp) water
- ¼ tsp rose water

7 Add the eggs in 3 goes, incorporating well after each addition. Add the sifted dry ingredients in 3–4 goes, folding in with a spatula or a large metal spoon, incorporating after each addition. Swirl in three-quarters of the apricot compôte. Spoon the batter into the prepared tin. Tap the tin gently on the worktop to release any air pockets.

8 Place the apricot halves on top of the batter, gently pushing them in. Sprinkle the extra 50g (¼ cup) sugar over the apricots.

9 Bake for 45–50 minutes. After 30 minutes cover with foil if it is browning too much. The cake is ready when the surface is springy to touch and a skewer comes out clean.

10 Cool the cake for 10 minutes in the tin, then turn out on a wire rack.

11 Warm the remaining compôte in a small pan with a couple of spoonfuls of water. Pass it through a sieve (strainer) to form a smooth glaze. Brush over the cake, then leave for an hour for the glaze to settle.

12 Dust with icing sugar, then scatter with sesame seeds and edible flowers.

To decorate (optional)

· icing (confectioners') sugar to dust

· sesame seeds, to sprinkle

· edible flowers

Plum, almond and saffron torte

This cake uses the all-in-one method (page 36) and is ready to eat as soon as it comes out of the oven. You can change the fruits and flavours with the seasons: in summer, dress it up with berries and whipped cream; in autumn, enjoy warm served with jugs of custard. Every time you change the fruit, it feels like a different cake! Cardamom and apricot, thyme and gooseberry, rhubarb and orange zest, figs and saffron... you get the idea.

1 Butter and flour a 20cm (8in) round cake tin, or use a springform or loose-bottom tin if you have one. Line the base and sides of the tin with a sheet of baking paper, allowing a 2cm (¾in) overhang. Preheat the oven to 160°C fan/180°C/350°F/Gas mark 4.

2 Cut each plum half into 4 equal slices.

3 Put the remaining cake ingredients, except the demerara sugar, in a large bowl if using a hand-held beater, or a stand mixer with a beater attachment. Beat on medium speed until you have a thick batter that is pale and fluffy – about 3–4 minutes.

4 Spoon the batter into the prepared tin. Arrange the sliced plums all around the cake in a circular pattern. Sprinkle the demerara sugar over the surface and plums.

5 Bake for 45 minutes, covering with foil after 30 minutes if it is browning too much, until a skewer comes out clean.

6 Cool the cake for 10 minutes in the tin, then turn out onto a wire rack.

7 While the cake is cooling, make the syrup. Put the sugar and water in a small pan over a medium heat. Cook for 5 minutes until honey-like in consistency. Remove from the heat and leave until it is lukewarm. Add the saffron and salt.

8 Once the cake has completely cooled, brush the warm saffron syrup over the surface and plums.

9 To serve, dust with icing sugar and sprinkle with toasted almond flakes.

10 Store at room temperature for 2 days, or for 3–4 days in the fridge.

- 150g (⅔ cup) butter, plus extra for greasing
- 150g (1 cup plus 2 Tbsp) plain (all-purpose) flour, plus extra for dusting
- 6–8 plums, halved and stoned
- 1½ tsp baking powder
- 150g (1½ cups) ground almonds
- 150g (¾ cup plus 1 Tbsp) golden caster (superfine) sugar
- 4 eggs
- ¼ tsp sea salt
- 1 tsp vanilla extract
- 10–12 saffron strands, crushed to a fine powder
- 4 Tbsp demerara (raw brown) sugar

For the saffron syrup

- 50g (¼ cup) golden caster (superfine) sugar
- 50ml (3 Tbsp plus 1 tsp) water
- 10–12 saffron strands
- pinch of salt

To decorate

- icing (confectioners') sugar
- toasted almond flakes

Peach crumble cake

I thought I loved peaches – then I tried the local peaches in Sicily. They had the most amazing texture and sweetness. Since then, no other peach has come close. In fact, we manage to come home from that trip with 6 kilos of them! On our way to the airport, a small lorry piled high with fresh peaches drove past us. I mentioned how much I loved them. The next thing I knew, our driver accelerated and almost pulled in front of the lorry, forcing the lorry driver to stop! He got out, negotiated a price of 2 euros for 6 kilos, and off we went like normal. That incident still makes me smile. We returned home with our spoils and that week I experimented with ice cream, compôte, crumble and this cake.

---

1 Begin with the crumble. Add all the ingredients to a bowl, then clump everything together, but do not overmix: a coarse, rubble-like texture is what we want. Put the crumble in a freezer bag and freeze until required.

Tip I always make a double batch! It freezes well, ready for a quick fruit crumble, or you can bake the crumble on a lined baking sheet to sprinkle on cake or desserts.

2 Butter and flour a 20cm (8in) round cake tin, or use a springform cake tin. Line the base and sides with a large sheet of baking paper with 2–3cm (about 1in) overhang. Preheat the oven to 170°C fan/190°C/375°F/Gas mark 5.

3 Chop 2 of the peaches into small pieces and thinly slice the other 2. Squeeze lemon juice over them all, to prevent discoloration.

4 Sift the flour, custard powder, baking powder and salt into a large bowl, then mix in the ground almonds.

5 Break the eggs into a small jug and stir so they are just mixed.

For the crumble

- 150g (1 cup plus 2 Tbsp) plain (all-purpose) flour
- 85g (½ cup) caster (superfine) sugar
- 125g (½ cup plus 1 Tbsp) butter
- 100g (1 cup) whole, unskinned almonds, roughly chopped
- 30g (2½ Tbsp) demerara (raw brown) sugar
- 30g (about 3 Tbsp) porridge oats (oatmeal)
- 1 tsp vanilla extract
- 1 Tbsp sea salt flakes

For the batter

- 175g (¾ cup plus 1 tsp) butter, plus extra for greasing
- 175g (1⅓ cups) plain (all-purpose) flour, plus extra for dusting
- 4 large fresh yellow peaches (or nectarines), halved and stoned
- zest and juice of 1 lemon
- 25g (3 Tbsp) custard powder (instant vanilla pudding) or cornflour (cornstarch)
- 1½ tsp baking powder
- ½ tsp salt
- 100g (1 cup) ground almonds
- 4 eggs
- 50ml (scant ¼ cup) extra virgin olive oil
- 225g (1 cup plus 2 Tbsp) golden caster (superfine) sugar
- ¼ tsp almond extract
- 1 tsp vanilla bean paste
- 5 Tbsp milk
- icing (confectioners') sugar, for dusting (optional)

6 Put the butter, oil, sugar, almond extract, vanilla and lemon zest into a large bowl if using a hand-held beater, or use a stand mixer. Beat until the mixture is pale and fluffy. Add the eggs in 3–4 goes, incorporating well after each addition. Add the sifted dry ingredients in 3–4 goes, gently folding in after each addition. Do not overmix. Fold in the chopped peaches and milk, and give it one last stir.

7 Spoon the batter into the prepared tin. Tap the tin gently on the worktop to release any air pockets. Arrange the sliced peaches over the batter, then top with the prepared crumble mixture.

8 Bake for 45–50 minutes, covering with foil after 30 minutes if it is browning too much, until a skewer comes out clean.

9 Cool the cake for 10 minutes in the tin, then turn out onto a wire rack. Finish with a dusting of icing sugar, if you wish.

10 This is good eaten warm, or at room temperature, served with custard as a pudding. It's best eaten on the day it's made.

Mango shrikhand cake

Shrikhand is a yoghurt dessert from India, flavoured with cardamom,
saffron and assorted nuts. It is somehow rich, creamy, light and delicate.
When Indian mangoes are in season, the chopped, fresh, sweet fruit
and tangy, nutty-flavoured yoghurt are well worth trying together.
Look for Kesar or Alphonso mangoes and use a strained Greek yoghurt
for the topping.

---

1 Butter and flour a 20cm (8in) round cake tin. Line the
base with a disc of baking paper. Preheat the oven to
170°C fan/190°C/375°F/Gas mark 5.

2 Sift the flour, baking powder and salt into a bowl.

3 Put the butter, milk, saffron and cardamom in a small pan.
Gently heat until the butter has melted: do not boil, keep it on
a simmer.

4 Put the eggs, yolks, sugar and vanilla in a large bowl,
if using a hand-held whisk, or a stand mixer with a whisk
attachment. Beat on a medium to high speed, until the
mixture is pale in colour and trebled in volume, about
6–8 minutes.

5 Add the sifted dry ingredients in 3–4 goes, gently folding in,
without deflating the batter.

6 Put 5–6 tablespoons of the batter into a small bowl and pour
in the hot milk and butter. Gently fold together: the batter
will melt but it will also temper the mixture so that the hot
liquid can be added to the remaining batter. Add this hot milk
mixture to the bowl of cake batter, gently folding it in.

7 Pour the batter into the prepared cake tin. Bake for
40–45 minutes, or until the surface is springy to touch and
a skewer comes out clean.

8 Cool the cake for 10 minutes in the tin, then turn out onto a
wire rack.

9 To make the shrikhand, put all the ingredients in a large
bowl and use a balloon whisk to mix everything together until
light and fluffy.

10 Once the cake has completely cooled, place it on a suitable
serving plate or a cake board. Dollop the shrikhand on top of
the cake, pile on the mangoes and finish with a sprinkle of
pistachio nibs and edible flowers.

11 Store for 3 days in the fridge.

- 100g (½ cup minus 1 Tbsp) butter,
  plus extra for greasing
- 220g (1⅔ cups) plain (all-purpose) flour,
  plus extra for dusting
- 2 tsp baking powder
- ¼ tsp salt
- 250ml (1 cup) milk
- 10–12 saffron strands
- 5–6 green cardamom pods, husks
  removed and seeds ground to
  a fine powder
- 3 eggs plus 2 egg yolks
- 340g (1¾ cups plus 2 Tbsp) golden caster
  (superfine) sugar
- 1 Tbsp vanilla bean paste

For the shrikhand
- 150g (½ cup) full-fat Greek yoghurt (hung
  for a few hours to drain excess water)
- 100ml (7 Tbsp) double (heavy) cream
- 10–12 saffron strands
- 25g (3½ Tbsp) sifted icing (confectioners')
  sugar
- ½ tsp salt
- 2–3 cardamom pods, husks removed and
  seeds ground to a fine powder

To decorate
- 2–3 Indian mangoes, peeled, stones
  removed, chopped into small pieces
- pistachio nibs
- edible flowers (optional)

Brown butter apple cake

There are thousands of varieties of apples in the world. My guess is that there are as many, if not more, apple cake recipes! Paired with brown butter, an amazing ingredient that gives a richer butter note to cakes (see page 46), this recipe tastes and smells like autumn on a plate.

1 Butter and flour a 20cm (8in) round cake tin. Line the base and sides with a large sheet of baking paper (see tip). Preheat the oven to 160°C fan/180°C/350°F/Gas mark 4.

2 Wash and core the apples (no need to peel them). Chop 2 into small pieces and cut the other 2 into long thin slices – use a mandoline if you have one. Squeeze lemon juice over them all, to prevent discoloration.

3 Sift the flour, baking powder and salt into a large bowl and mix in the ground almonds.

4 Put the eggs, vanilla and golden caster and light brown soft sugars in a large bowl if using a hand-held whisk, or use a stand mixer with a whisk attachment. Whisk until pale, thick and doubled in volume.

5 Gently fold the flour mixture into the egg mixture in 2–3 goes, using a large metal spoon. Try to maintain as much volume in the batter as possible. Gently pour in the melted brown butter and cream, then add the lemon zest. Give it a couple of gentle stirs and then fold in the chopped apples.

6 Pour the batter into the prepared tin. Tap the tin gently on the worktop to release any air pockets. Arrange the sliced apples over the batter to form a concentric pattern, overlapping the slices slightly, and sprinkle the demerara sugar over them.

7 Bake for 45–50 minutes. After 30 minutes cover with foil if it is browning too much. The cake is ready when the surface is springy to touch and a skewer comes out clean.

8 Cool the cake for 10 minutes in the tin, then carefully turn out onto a wire rack.

9 Once cooled, brush the top of the cake with warm honey or apricot jam to give the cake a shine.

Tip

A springform or a loose-bottom tin is useful in this recipe for the ease of demoulding. However, if you don't have either, use a large piece of baking paper and allow a slight overhang to lift it out.

- butter, for greasing
- 175g (1⅓ cups) plain (all-purpose) flour, plus extra for dusting
- 4 eating apples, such as Cox or Braeburn
- zest and juice of 1 lemon
- 1½ tsp baking powder
- ¼ tsp salt
- 75g (¾ cup) ground almonds
- 4 eggs
- 1 tsp vanilla bean paste
- 125g (⅔ cup) golden caster (superfine) sugar
- 100g (about ½ cup) light soft brown sugar
- 200g (¾ cup plus 2 Tbsp) Brown Butter (page 46), from 250g (1 cup plus 2 Tbsp) butter, melted and slightly cooled
- 75g (¼ cup plus 1 Tbsp) soured cream
- 50g (4 Tbsp) demerara (raw brown) sugar, for sprinkling
- 75g (4 Tbsp) honey or apricot jam (jelly), warmed, to glaze

Fig, walnut and honey cake

Fresh figs have a short season but are worth seeking out: look for deep-purple outsides and ruby red insides. I made this cake for my neighbour, Esther, to take to her Jordanian family, as these flavours are abundant in the Middle East. Make this cake as a dessert, or just serve with a nice cup of tea.

1 Brush a 20cm (8in) round cake tin with olive oil and dust with flour. Line the base with a disc of baking paper. Preheat the oven to 170°C fan/190°C/375°F/Gas mark 5.

2 Sift the flour, baking powder, polenta and salt into a large bowl and add the walnuts.

3 Put the eggs into another large bowl if using a hand-held mixer, or use a stand mixer with a whisk attachment, and whisk for 2 minutes. Add the sugar, olive oil, lemon zest, vanilla, orange blossom water and honey. Mix it for a further few minutes until well combined. Do not overmix.

4 Add the sifted dry ingredients in 2–3 goes, followed by the yoghurt or soured cream, using a spatula or large metal spoon to fold it in. Do not overmix – stop when the dry and wet ingredients are combined.

5 Pour the batter into the prepared tin. Tap the tin gently on the worktop to release any air pockets. Bake for 40–45 minutes, covering with foil after 30 minutes if it is browning too much, until a skewer comes out clean.

6 Meanwhile, prepare the figs. Quarter each one but don't cut through the base. Place in a single layer in a small non-stick frying pan (skillet) and drizzle with honey. Cook over a gentle heat for 5–6 minutes until they are slightly soft and yielding. Turn off the heat and set aside.

7 Whisk the mascarpone with the honey. Place in the fridge.

8 Once the cake is baked, let it cool for 10 minutes in the tin, then turn out onto a wire rack.

9 Once the cake is completely cool, place it on a serving plate or cake stand. Top with the mascarpone, then pile high with figs, a drizzle of the honey juices from the pan and the chopped walnuts.

10 Sprinkle with edible flowers if you wish.

11 Keep for 2–3 days in the fridge.

- 120ml (½ cup plus 1 Tbsp) olive oil, plus extra for greasing
- 150g (1 cup plus 2 Tbsp) plain (all-purpose) flour, plus extra for dusting
- 1½ tsp baking powder
- 75g (½ cup) fine polenta
- ¼ tsp salt
- 100g (about 1 cup) walnuts, lightly toasted and finely chopped
- 4 eggs
- 100g (½ cup) light soft brown sugar
- zest of 2 lemons
- ½ tsp vanilla bean extract
- ¼ tsp orange blossom water
- 75g (4 Tbsp) honey
- 75g (about ¼ cup) Greek yoghurt or soured cream

For the glazed figs
- 6 fresh figs
- 50g (3 Tbsp) honey

To finish
- 250g (1 cup plus 1 Tbsp) mascarpone
- 35–50g (2–3 Tbsp) honey (orange blossom, if available), to taste
- 50g (about ½ cup) walnuts, lightly toasted and finely chopped
- edible flowers (optional)

Chocolate, pear and hazelnut cake

Some flavour combinations are classics and this is one of them. This cake makes a lovely warm dessert served with salted caramel or vanilla ice cream. It's equally good – hot or cold – with a cup of coffee. I confess I may have eaten leftovers for breakfast a few times. Yes, it is that good!

Don't be tempted to skip roasting the hazelnuts as this gives better flavour and texture to the cake.

1 Begin with the pears. Cut each half into 3. Put the butter and sugar in a large frying pan (skillet) over a medium heat. Once the butter has melted and the sugar dissolved, add the lemon juice, vanilla and salt. Place the pears in a single layer in the pan (or cook in 2 batches if your pan is small) and cook gently until the pears are just cooked – they should still hold their shape and look glossy. This takes about 10–12 minutes, depending on their ripeness.

Tip The cooked pears can be stored in the fridge for up to 3 days. Store in a suitable container with any juices left in the pan. Bring them to room temperature before using.

2 Put the hazelnuts in a small dry frying pan and roast over a medium heat, stirring them continuously for 10–12 minutes. Alternatively, roast them at 160°C fan/180°C/350°F/Gas mark 4 for 10–12 minutes. Keep an eye on them – they burn easily! Turn off the heat and spread the hot hazelnuts on a clean tea (dish) towel. Vigorously rub the towel around the hazelnuts and most of the skins should fall off – don't worry if some remain. Set aside 10 hazelnuts. Blitz the rest in a food processor or finely chop by hand. Alternatively place them in a food-safe bag and smash with a rolling pin.

3 Butter and flour a 20cm (8in) springform cake tin. Line the base of the tin with a disc of baking paper. Preheat the oven to 160°C fan/180°C/350°F/Gas mark 4.

4 Sift the flour, cocoa powder and salt into a bowl and stir through the blitzed roasted hazelnuts.

5 Break the eggs into a small jug or bowl and gently mix with a fork.

For the pears

- 4–5 pears (slightly underripe is best), peeled, halved and cored
- 75g (⅓ cup) butter
- 50g (about ¼ cup) soft brown sugar
- 1 Tbsp lemon juice
- 1 tsp vanilla bean paste
- ¼ tsp salt

For the batter

- 175g (¾ cup plus 1 tsp) butter, plus extra for greasing
- 125g (1 cup minus 1 Tbsp) self-raising (self-rising) flour, plus extra for dusting
- 125g (about 1 cup) unskinned hazelnuts
- 50g (about ½ cup) cocoa powder
- ¼ tsp salt
- 3 eggs
- 175g (1 cup) caster (superfine) sugar
- ½ tsp vanilla extract

6 Put the butter and sugar in a large bowl if using a hand-held beater, or a stand mixer with a beater attachment. Beat on a medium speed for 4–5 minutes, or until light and pale. Now add the vanilla and give a quick stir.

7 Add the beaten eggs in 3–4 goes, incorporating well after each addition. Now add in the sifted dry ingredients in 3–4 goes, gently folding in after each addition.

8 Pour the batter into the prepared tin and spread it in an even layer. Give the tin a gentle tap on the counter to release any trapped air. Arrange the prepared pears around the edge of the batter, packing them closely together.

9 Bake on the middle shelf of the oven for 40 minutes. Test by inserting a skewer: it should come out clean. If still not cooked, cover with foil and cook for a further 10 minutes.

10 Place the cake on a cooling rack for 10 minutes before turning out of the tin.

11 Sprinkle with the reserved toasted hazelnuts, keeping some whole and some cut in halves. Enjoy warm or cold.

Pistachio and blood orange cake

This cake is inspired by the foothills of Mount Etna, where I saw pistachio trees and orange trees growing side by side in the volcanic soil. Blood oranges are mellow, fragrant and sweet, and don't have the sharp tang of other citrus fruits. There are several varieties but the delicate-flavoured Moro has a deeper red flesh and its orange skin is speckled with red. Out of season, you can make this with ordinary oranges.

1 Butter and line a 20cm (8in) round cake tin with baking paper. Preheat the oven to 170°C fan/190°C/375°F/Gas mark 5.

2 Sift the flour, baking powder, salt and ground cardamom into a large bowl, then add the ground pistachios.

3 Break the eggs into a jug. Stir with a fork until just mixed.

4 Put the butter, sugar, citrus zests and vanilla in another large bowl if using a hand-held beater, or use a stand mixer with a beater attachment. Beat on a medium speed for 6–8 minutes, or until pale and fluffy.

5 Add the eggs in 3–4 goes, incorporating well each time.

6 Alternately fold in the sifted dry ingredients and the soured cream in 3–4 goes until just combined to a smooth batter. Do not overmix.

7 Pour the batter into the prepared tin. Tap the tin gently on the worktop to release any air pockets. Bake for 35–40 minutes. Test by inserting a skewer: it should come out clean. If it is not, cover with foil and cook for a further 5–10 minutes.

8 Meanwhile, make the syrup. Weigh the juice from the fruit, then pour into a small pan over a medium heat. Add an equal weight of sugar and the pinch of salt. Simmer until the sugar dissolves completely and continue to cook for 3–5 minutes until a thin syrup forms – you don't want it to be thick. Remove from the heat and set aside.

9 When the cake is baked, leave it in the tin to cool for 10 minutes. Then poke holes over the surface with a skewer and brush half the syrup over the top.

10 After 10 minutes turn out the cake from the tin and place on a wire rack. Brush the remaining syrup on the sides as well.

11 Once the cake is cold, mix the ingredients for the glaze, if using, to a pouring consistency. Add the juice sparingly: you may not need all of it. Pour over the cake and, if you wish, add a sprinkle of chopped pistachios and edible flowers.

- 175g (¾ cup plus 1 tsp) butter, plus extra for greasing
- 175g (1⅓ cups) self-raising (self-rising) flour, plus extra for dusting
- 1½ tsp baking powder
- ¼ tsp salt
- 4–5 green cardamom pods, husks removed and seeds ground to a powder
- 120g (generous 1 cup) finely ground pistachio nuts
- 4 eggs
- 175g (1 cup) golden caster (superfine) sugar
- zest of 3 blood oranges (juice reserved for the syrup)
- zest of 1 lemon (juice reserved for the syrup)
- 1 tsp vanilla extract
- 50g (scant ¼ cup) soured cream

For the syrup
- juice of 3 blood oranges
- juice of 1 lemon
- caster sugar – the same amount by weight of sugar to juice
- pinch of sea salt

For the sugar glaze (optional)
- 150g (1¼ cups) sifted icing (confectioners') sugar
- 3 Tbsp blood orange juice, or as needed
- pinch of sea salt

To decorate (optional)
- pistachio nibs
- edible flowers

White chocolate and raspberry cake

On its own, white chocolate can be overly sweet, but its subtle flavour enhances the vanilla in the batter and gives a softer crumb, similar to brownies. Here it pairs well with the tartness of the raspberries. Freeze-dried raspberry powder adds colour and flavour.

1 Butter and flour a 20cm (8in) round cake tin. Line the sides and base with baking paper. Preheat the oven to 170°C fan/190°C/375°F/Gas mark 5.

2 Sift the flour, baking powder and salt into a large bowl.

3 Break the eggs into a small jug or bowl and stir with a fork.

4 In another jug or small bowl, mix the melted white chocolate, double cream and lemon juice.

5 Put the butter, lemon zest, sugar and vanilla in a large bowl if using a hand-held beater, or use a stand mixer with a beater attachment. Beat for 7–8 minutes on a medium speed until pale and fluffy. Add the eggs in 3–4 goes, incorporating well after each addition.

6 Fold in the sifted dry ingredients and the white chocolate mixture in 3–4 goes, alternating between them.

7 Spoon half the batter into another bowl. Add the freeze-dried raspberry powder to one of the batters. Give it a gentle stir until it turns pink.

8 Spoon the plain batter and raspberry batter alternately into the prepared cake tin, then create a marble pattern using a skewer (see page 65). Push the fresh raspberries into the batter. Bake for 40–45 minutes, or until the surface is springy to touch and a skewer comes out clean.

9 Let the cake cool in the tin for 10 minutes, then turn out onto a wire rack to cool completely.

10 Meanwhile, make the glaze. Mix together the ingredients, using enough lemon juice for a thick pourable consistency. Pour the glaze over the cake and leave to set. Alternatively, scatter with edible flowers before the icing sets completely.

11 For optional further decoration, when the glaze is set, melt some white chocolate and drizzle it over the cake and sprinkle with extra freeze-dried raspberry powder and edible flowers.

- 185g (¾ cup plus 1 Tbsp) butter, plus extra for greasing
- 225g (about 1¾ cups) plain (all-purpose) flour, plus extra for dusting
- 2 tsp baking powder
- ½ tsp salt
- 4 large eggs
- 200g (7oz) white chocolate, melted (page 19)
- 125ml (½ cup) double (heavy) cream
- zest and juice of 1 lemon
- 200g (generous 1 cup) golden caster (superfine) sugar
- 1 Tbsp vanilla bean paste
- 30g (2 Tbsp) sifted freeze-dried raspberry powder (optional)
- 100g (scant 1 cup) fresh raspberries

For the glaze
- 250g (2 cups plus 2 Tbsp) sifted icing (confectioners') sugar
- 50g (5 Tbsp) sifted freeze-dried raspberry powder
- 3–4 Tbsp lemon juice
- pinch of salt

To decorate (optional)
- 75g (2½oz) white chocolate, melted (page 19)
- freeze-dried raspberry powder
- edible flowers

Lime and mint cake

I don't drink alcohol but I love a virgin mojito. It is my drink of choice, a refreshing concoction of lime, mint and brown sugar. If you like citrus, you will love this cake. In summer, I make it for picnics and garden parties.

---

1 Butter and flour a 20cm (8in) round cake tin. Line the base with a disc of baking paper. Preheat the oven to 170°C fan/190°C/375°F/Gas mark 5.

2 Sift the flour, baking powder, salt and ground almonds into a large bowl.

3 Break the eggs into a small jug and stir with a fork until just mixed.

4 In another small bowl or jug, mix the soured cream, lime zest and juice.

5 Put the butter, sugar and vanilla in another large bowl if using a hand-held mixer, or use a stand mixer with a beater attachment, and beat for at least 6–7 minutes on medium speed until the mixture is pale and fluffy. Add the eggs in 3–4 goes, incorporating well after each addition.

6 Alternately fold in the sifted dry ingredients and the soured cream and lime mixture in 3–4 goes until just combined to a smooth batter. Do not overmix.

7 Spoon the batter into the prepared tin and give it a sharp tap on the counter to release any air bubbles.

8 Bake on the middle shelf of the oven for 40–45 minutes. After 30 minutes cover with foil if it is browning too much. The cake is ready when the surface is springy to touch and a skewer comes out clean.

9 Cool the cake for 10 minutes in the tin, then turn out onto a wire rack.

10 While the cake is baking, make the mint syrup. Put the sugar, water, lime juice and salt in a small pan over a medium heat. Keep on a gentle simmer until the sugar dissolves completely. Cook for a further 5 minutes on a gentle heat, then turn off the heat. Allow to cool for 10 minutes, then add the lime zest and fresh mint leaves. Leave to infuse while the cake is in the oven (about 45 minutes), then strain through a fine strainer into a bowl, discarding the mint leaves.

- 200g (¾ cup plus 2 Tbsp) butter, plus extra for greasing
- 200g (1½ cups) plain (all-purpose) flour, plus extra for dusting
- 1½ tsp baking powder
- ½ tsp salt
- 100g (1 cup) ground almonds
- 4 eggs
- 75g (about ¼ cup) soured cream
- zest and juice of 4 limes
- 200g (1 cup) light soft brown sugar
- ½ tsp vanilla extract

For the mint syrup

- 100g (generous ½ cup) caster (superfine) sugar
- 75ml (5 Tbsp) water
- zest and juice of 2 limes
- ½ tsp salt
- 15–20 fresh mint leaves

For the glaze

- 200g (1¾ cups) sifted icing (confectioners') sugar
- zest and juice of 1 lime
- pinch of salt

To decorate

- a few sprigs of mint
- edible flowers (optional)
- 1 lime, thinly sliced

11 Brush the syrup all over the warm cake, including the sides. Brush it a few times, then leave to soak in. You may not need all the syrup: leftovers can be used for mojitos or lemonade.

12 To make the glaze, stir the ingredients together and gradually add 1–2 tablespoons of water – you want a thick pouring consistency, so add the water sparingly. Cover and set aside.

13 Once the cake has completely cooled, pour over the glaze to completely cover it. Leave for 10 minutes. While the glaze is still wet, decorate with mint sprigs, edible flowers and thin slices of lime.

Cakes from around the world

It was only through marriage, when I moved to London and began to travel more, that I learned there was more to the world of cake than marble cake and pineapple upside-down cake! Every home, every region, every country around the globe transforms the basics of flour, fat, eggs and sugar into a moment of happiness.

The cakes in this chapter require a little more skill and confidence. They take more time, effort and involve multiple techniques. I urge you to read the recipes thoroughly before attempting them, and to source quality ingredients.

By travelling the world from your kitchen, you will build on your exploration of flavour and expand your cake repertoire. A world of flavour awaits you!

Australian lamington

A cake coated in jam and covered in desiccated coconut is my idea of delicious. When I first came across a lamington recipe, I had to read it twice as it explained that the sauce – originally chocolate sauce – had to be spread on the outside of the cake. My version is sandwiched with and covered in passion fruit curd, then finished with desiccated and flaked coconut and white chocolate shards. Use any jam or fruit curd you like.

1 Butter and flour a 20cm (8in) round cake tin. Line the base with a disc of baking paper. Preheat the oven to 160°C fan/180°C/350°F/Gas mark 4.

2 Sift the flour, baking powder and salt into a large bowl.

3 Put the lime zest and the sugar into a large bowl, if using a hand-held whisk, or a stand mixer with a whisk attachment. Using your hands, rub the zest into the sugar to infuse it with flavour. Add the eggs to the bowl and whisk on a medium to high speed until tripled in volume and pale in colour.

4 Sift in the flour mixture in 3–4 goes, gently folding in after each addition with a metal spoon to avoid deflating the batter. Fold in the vanilla and desiccated coconut.

5 Put a couple of spoonfuls of this batter in a medium bowl and mix it with the melted butter. Use the whisk to fold this butter mixture back into the bowl of batter and give it a quick stir until combined.

6 Pour the cake batter into the prepared tin. Tap the tin gently on the worktop to release any air pockets. Bake for 45–50 minutes, covering with foil after 30 minutes if it is browning too much. The cake is ready when the surface is springy to touch and a skewer comes out clean.

7 Cool the cake for 10 minutes in the tin, then turn out onto a wire rack and let it cool completely.

8 Cut the cake horizontally into 2 discs.

9 Place one of the cake layers on a cake board or plate. Spread the passion fruit curd for the filling evenly on the cake. Top with the second layer of cake.

10 To finish, spread passion fruit curd over the sides and top of the sandwiched cake. Sprinkle the desiccated coconut and coconut flakes all over the curd.

11 Let it set completely. Decorate with edible flowers and white chocolate shards (see right).

- 50g (3½ Tbsp) butter, melted and cooled, plus extra for greasing
- 200g (1½ cups) plain (all-purpose) flour, plus extra for dusting
- 1 tsp baking powder
- ¼ tsp salt
- zest of 2 limes
- 200g (generous 1 cup) golden caster (superfine) sugar
- 5 eggs
- 1 tsp vanilla bean paste
- 150g (about 2 cups) desiccated (shredded) coconut

For the filling

- 75g (2¾oz) passion fruit curd (available online)

To finish

- 100g (3½oz) passion fruit curd
- 150g (about 2 cups) desiccated (shredded) coconut and coconut flakes

Chocolate shards (see below)

- 100g (3½oz) white chocolate, melted (page 19)
- 50g (about 1 cup) coconut flakes
- 1 Tbsp coconut oil or sunflower oil
- edible flowers

To make chocolate shards

Add the coconut oil or sunflower oil to the melted chocolate and mix. Place a sheet of baking paper on a tray. Pour the melted chocolate on the paper and spread it into a thin layer. Add edible flowers and petals and some of the coconut flakes. Put the tray in the fridge until the chocolate has completely hardened. Once set, break into large pieces and use to decorate the cake.

Citronmåne ('lemon moon' cake)

Citronmåne is a Danish lemon and almond cake cut in half, in the shape of a half moon. Without knowing this, I would often divide cakes this way, saving half for home and sharing the other half with friends, family and neighbours. I once took a lemon cake, cut like this, to a friend's house. Her au pair saw the cake and said it was a lemon moon cake! I hadn't heard of one before so I did some research and played around with my recipe, adding almonds to it. I have never eaten a Danish citronmåne but I think this might come close.

1 Butter and flour a 20cm (8in) round cake tin. Line the base with a disc of baking paper. Preheat the oven to 170°C fan/190°C/375°F/Gas mark 5.

2 Sift the flour, cornflour, baking powder and salt into a large bowl and mix in the ground almonds.

3 Break the eggs and yolks into a small jug and stir with a fork.

4 Put the butter, sugar, lemon zest and vanilla in a large bowl if using a hand-held beater, or a stand mixer with a beater attachment. Cream for about 6–8 minutes until pale and fluffy. Add the eggs in 3–4 goes, beating after each addition. Sift in the dry ingredients in 3–4 goes and gently fold in after each addition. Add the lemon juice and fold in.

5 Pour the batter into the prepared tin. Add a few dollops of the lemon curd on top of the batter. Using a skewer, swirl the lemon curd into the batter. Give the tin a sharp tap on the worktop to release any air pockets.

6 Bake for 40–45 minutes. After 30 minutes cover with foil if it is browning too much. The cake is ready when the surface is springy to touch and a skewer comes out clean.

7 Cool the cake for 10 minutes in the tin, then turn out onto a wire rack.

8 To make the icing, mix the icing sugar, lemon juice, vanilla and salt to a thick consistency. If it seems too thick add a little water – go cautiously.

9 Pour the icing over the cooled cake. Decorate with almond flakes and edible flowers, if you wish. Once the icing has completely set, use a sharp knife to cut the cake in half.

10 Keep half for yourself, or – if you are mad on lemon cake like me – keep it all to yourself and enjoy over 5 days.

- 200g (¾ cup plus 2 Tbsp) butter, plus extra for greasing
- 200g (1½ cups) plain (all-purpose) flour, plus extra for dusting
- 25g (¼ cup) cornflour (cornstarch)
- 1 tsp baking powder
- ½ tsp salt
- 200g (2 cups) ground almonds
- 3 eggs plus 2 egg yolks
- 200g (generous 1 cup) golden caster (superfine) sugar
- zest and juice of 3 lemons
- 1 tsp vanilla bean paste
- 3 Tbsp Lemon Curd (page 48)

For the icing (frosting)

- 200g (1¾ cups) sifted icing (confectioners') sugar
- juice of 1 lemon
- ¼ tsp vanilla bean paste
- ¼ tsp salt
- 2–3 tsp water, as required

To decorate (optional)

- almond flakes
- white and yellow edible flowers

Italian ricotta citrus cake

This cake uses fresh ricotta and is based on a cake I had on a Sicilian holiday. I just couldn't get enough of it – I ate it every day of our trip! It was comforting, light, soft, lemony and delicious, with a sugary crust. It reminds me of Sicily, where streets are lined with lemon and ancient olive trees, and food is a language spoken passionately.

If we have guests, I sometimes bake this as part of a summer breakfast, served with Greek yoghurt and orange blossom honey. If you only bake one recipe from this chapter, make it this one.

1 Oil and flour a 20cm (8in) round cake tin, or use a springform tin. Line the base and sides with a large piece of baking paper allowing it to overhang. Preheat the oven to 160°C fan/180°C/ 350°F/Gas mark 4.

2 Tip the ricotta into a sieve (strainer) and leave for 15 minutes for any excess liquid to drain away, otherwise the cake may be soggy.

3 Sift the flour, baking powder, bicarbonate of soda and salt into a large bowl. Mix in the ground almonds.

4 Put the olive oil, golden caster sugar and eggs in another large bowl if using a hand-held beater, or a stand mixer with a beater attachment. Whisk for 1 minute, then add the strained ricotta, the citrus zest and juices, the vanilla and almond extract, and give it a good mix.

5 Now sift in the dry ingredients in 3–4 goes, folding in with a large metal spoon until fully combined. Stir through the candied (mixed) citrus peel.

6 Pour the batter into the prepared tin. Tap the tin gently on the worktop to release any air pockets. Sprinkle the extra caster sugar to form an even layer on top of the batter.

7 Bake for 45–50 minutes. After 30 minutes cover with foil if it is browning too much. The cake is ready when a lovely crackly crust has developed and a skewer comes out clean.

8 Cool the cake for 10 minutes in the tin, then turn out onto a wire rack and let the cake cool completely.

9 This cake is best eaten on the day it is made, either warm or cold. It will still be delicious after 2–3 days, although the sugary crust will soften slightly.

- 120ml (½ cup) extra virgin olive oil, plus extra for greasing
- 150g (1 cup plus 2 Tbsp) plain (all-purpose) flour, plus extra for dusting
- 300g (1¼ cups plus 1 Tbsp) ricotta
- 1½ tsp baking powder
- ½ tsp bicarbonate of soda (baking soda)
- ½ tsp salt
- 100g (1 cup) ground almonds
- 150g (¾ cup plus 1 Tbsp) golden caster (superfine) sugar, plus 50g (generous ¼ cup) for sprinkling
- 3 eggs
- zest and juice of 1 large lemon
- zest and juice of 1 large orange
- 1 tsp vanilla bean paste
- ¼ tsp almond extract
- 150g (scant 1¼ cups) candied (mixed) peel, chopped

To decorate (optional)

- icing (confectioners') sugar
- 3 or 4 candied orange slices
- edible flowers

Optional

For such a flavour-packed cake, once baked, it looks very simple. To dress it up, dust some icing (confectioners') sugar on the edges and place some candied orange slices and a scattering of edible flowers on top, if you wish.

German Black Forest cake

This is another much-loved chocolate cake, with its delicate chocolate sponge layers and generous filling of cherries and cream. Pâtisseries all over the world have a version of this, and it has been a staple for decades. Traditionally this is made with Genoise sponge but my version is flour-free (and therefore gluten-free) and incredibly light to eat. Use in-season cherries to make this that bit more special, or use a good-quality compôte.

1 Brush two 20cm (8in) round cake tins with butter. Line the base and sides with baking paper. Preheat the oven to 170°C fan/190°C/375°F/Gas mark 5.

2 To make the ganache, follow the method on page 51.

3 To make the filling, whip together all the ingredients in a bowl. Place in the fridge while you make the cake.

4 Put the egg whites in a large, perfectly clean bowl, if using a hand-held whisk, or a stand mixer with the whisk attachment. Whisk to soft peaks. Set aside. In another large bowl, whisk the egg yolks, sugar, salt and vanilla for 3–4 minutes until the mixture starts to turn fluffy and pale. Gently fold the cocoa powder into the yolk mixture.

5 Gently fold the meringue into the yolk mixture in 3–4 goes, combining carefully. Try not to deflate the batter.

6 Pour the batter equally into the prepared tins. Tap the tins gently on the worktop to release any air pockets. Bake in the oven for 18–22 minutes. Once out of the oven they will deflate slightly, but that's okay. Let the cakes cool for 10 minutes in the tins then turn out onto a wire rack and let cool completely.

7 Using a serrated knife, slice the cakes horizontally into 2 discs.

To assemble the cake

8 Line the tin with 2 layers of cling film (plastic wrap), allowing a slight overhang. Place one cake disc at the base of the tin. Brush it with some syrup. Then add a layer of ganache – about one-third – followed by one-third of the cream filling. Dollop on a few spoonfuls of cherry compôte and a few cherries.

9 Repeat the layering process, finishing with a layer of cake. Pull in all the cling film over the cake and place in the fridge to chill for 6–8 hours.

10 Once ready to serve, carefully lift the cake out of the tin using the cling film. Remove all the cling film and place the cake on a plate or cake stand. Dollop the whipped cream on top of the cake. Decorate with chocolate shavings, a few fresh cherries and edible flowers.

- butter, for greasing
- 6 eggs, separated
- 125g (⅔ cup) caster (superfine) sugar
- ¼ tsp salt
- 1 tsp vanilla extract
- 60g (generous ½ cup) cocoa powder, sifted
- 100ml (7 Tbsp) Sugar Syrup (page 46)

For the ganache layer
- 100g (3½oz) dark chocolate (70% cocoa), finely chopped
- 100g (3½oz) milk chocolate, finely chopped
- 200ml (¾ cup plus 1 Tbsp) double (heavy) cream

For the filling
- 500ml (1¾ cups plus 3 Tbsp) double (heavy) cream
- 25g (3½ Tbsp) sifted icing (confectioners') sugar
- 1 Tbsp vanilla bean paste

For the cherry layer
- 100g (about ⅓ cup) cherry compôte or cherry jam (jelly)
- 150g (about 1 cup) fresh cherries, stoned and halved

To decorate
- 200g (¾ cup) whipping cream whipped
- 200g (7oz) chocolate shavings
- fresh cherries
- edible flowers (optional)

Persian love cake

I have come across many recipes for love cake – some scented with rose and orange blossom water, some fragrant with spices like cardamom and aniseed. The proportion of nuts varies. I have tried to incorporate and balance fragrance, texture and spices in this version, my ode to all things Persian and the Spice Route.

---

1 Butter and flour a 20cm (8in) round cake tin. Line the base with a disc of baking paper. Preheat the oven to 170°C fan/190°C/375°F/Gas mark 5.

2 Sift the flour, baking powder, ground cardamom, nutmeg and salt into a large bowl. Stir in the ground pistachios.

3 Break the eggs into a small jug and stir until they are just mixed.

4 Put the butter, sugar, rose water and vanilla in a large bowl if using a hand-held beater, or a stand mixer with a beater attachment. Beat until the mixture is fluffy and pale. Add the eggs in 3–4 goes, incorporating them well after each addition.

5 Add the dry ingredients in 3–4 goes, folding gently after each addition. Add the soured cream and saffron water. Give everything a final fold.

6 Pour the batter into the prepared tin. Tap the tin gently on the worktop to release any air pockets. Bake for 45 minutes. After 30 minutes cover with foil if it is browning too much. The cake is ready when the surface is springy to touch and a skewer comes out clean.

7 Cool the cake for 10 minutes in the tin, then turn out onto a wire rack and leave to cool completely.

8 Meanwhile, make the glaze by mixing the icing sugar, rose water, saffron and milk to a thick pouring consistency – add 1–2 teaspoons of water if needed.

9 Once the cake is completely cooled, pour the vibrant yellow glaze over the cake.

10 Sprinkle with pistachio nibs and edible flowers – roses work well here.

- 200g (¾ cup plus 2 Tbsp) butter, plus extra for greasing
- 175g (1⅓ cups) plain (all-purpose) flour, plus extra for dusting
- 2 tsp baking powder
- ½ tsp ground cardamom
- 1 tsp freshly grated nutmeg
- ¼ tsp salt
- 150g (generous 1 cup) pistachios, ground to a fine powder
- 4 eggs
- 200g (generous 1 cup) golden caster (superfine) sugar
- 1 tsp rose water
- 1 tsp vanilla extract
- 50g (3 Tbsp) soured cream
- 10–12 saffron strands, lightly crushed and mixed with 1 Tbsp water

For the glaze

- 150g (1¼ cups) icing (confectioners') sugar
- ¼ tsp rose water
- 10–12 saffron strands, crushed to powder
- 4 Tbsp milk

To decorate

- pistachio nibs
- edible flowers

Sicilian cassata cake

Another Sicilian recipe. Maybe because I fell in love with Sicily, or perhaps because there is a place called Taormina – similar to my name, Tarunima. I think I left a bit of my heart there: it's a beautiful hilltown with cobblestone streets and a Roman amphitheatre, surrounded by blue waters. Vibrant, festive cassata cakes sit like jewel-encrusted crowns in the many pasticceria and bakery windows. This recipe is based on my memories of those cakes, with some of my twists and decorations.

1 The day before serving, prepare the fruit for the filling. Put the 200ml (¾ cup plus 1 Tbsp) orange juice and all the chopped fruit into a small pan over a low heat. Simmer for 5–7 minutes, then turn off the heat. Leave the fruits to soak overnight (or for at least 6 hours).

2 Butter a 20cm (8in) cake tin and line the base with a disc of baking paper. Preheat the oven to 165°C fan/185°C/360°F/ Gas mark 4½.

3 Sift the flour and salt into a large bowl and mix in the ground pistachios.

4 In another large bowl, if using a hand-held whisk, or a stand mixer with a whisk attachment, whisk the eggs and sugar for 6–8 minutes on a medium to high speed, or until trebled in volume. Once fluffy and pale, add the vanilla followed by the sifted dry ingredients, gently folding in using a large metal spoon until no flour streaks remain. Add the sunflower oil, pouring from the side of the bowl, and fold in gently and carefully to avoid deflating the batter.

5 Pour the batter into the prepared tin. Tap the tin gently on the worktop to release any air pockets. Bake for 35–40 minutes, or until the surface is springy to touch and a skewer comes out clean.

6 Leave the cake in the tin for 10 minutes to cool slightly, then gently turn out onto a wire rack and remove the baking paper. Once the cake has completely cooled, slice the cake horizontally into 4 thin discs. Keep wrapped until needed. Wash and dry the tin ready for assembling the cake later.

7 For the filling, put the ricotta, mascarpone and icing sugar in a large bowl and whisk using a balloon whisk. Add in the soaked fruits, chopped pistachios, chocolate, orange blossom water, vanilla extract, lemon and orange zests. Give everything a good mix until well combined.

- butter, for greasing
- 150g (1 cup plus 2 Tbsp) self-raising flour
- ¼ salt
- 100g (about 1 cup) ground pistachios (see page 19)
- 5 large eggs
- 150g (¾ cup plus 1 Tbsp) golden caster (superfine) sugar
- ½ tsp vanilla bean paste
- 50ml (scant ¼ cup) sunflower oil

For the filling

- 200ml (¾ cup plus 1 Tbsp) orange juice, and an extra 100ml (7 Tbsp)
- 50g (1¾oz) glacé cherries
- 100g (3½oz) dried mango, chopped
- 100g (3½oz) candied (mixed) peel, chopped
- 100g (3½oz) candied or glacé fruits like figs, pears and whole small oranges, chopped (optional)
- 600g (2½ cups plus 2 Tbsp) ricotta
- 200g (¾ plus 2 Tbsp) mascarpone cheese
- 75g (½ cup plus 1 Tbsp) sifted icing (confectioners') sugar
- 75g (generous ½ cup) coarsely chopped pistachio nuts
- 100g (3½oz) dark chocolate, chopped into small pieces
- ½ tsp orange blossom water (optional)
- 1 tsp vanilla extract
- zest of 1 lemon, plus the juice for the glaze (see opposite)
- zest of 1 orange

Assembly

8 Line a 20cm (8in) cake tin, or a springform cake tin, with 2 layers of cling film, leaving a ¾ in (2cm) overhang.

9 Place one of the cake discs in the base of the tin and brush generously using some of the 100ml (7 Tbsp) orange juice. Add a third of the ricotta and fruit mix over the sponge and level it.

10 Repeat so you are left with a cake disc on top. Brush it with the remaining orange juice.

11 Cover the cake with cling film and refrigerate for at least 24 hours.

12 Once completely chilled, ease the cake out of the tin and remove all the cling film. Transfer the cake to a serving plate or cake stand. Neaten the sides, if necessary, using a palette knife dipped in warm water.

To decorate the cake

13 Before pouring the glaze, chill the cake well by freezing for half an hour.

14 Mix the icing sugar, salt and enough lemon juice to make a thick pouring glaze.

15 Pour the glaze on top of the cake. Before it sets completely, decorate the cake with candied and glacé fruits.

16 Decorate the cake with candied and glace fruits with edible flowers. The brighter the better.

Tip Good-quality candied and crystallized fruits from Italian delis make all the difference.

For the glaze and decoration

· 200g (1¾ cups) sifted icing (confectioners') sugar
· pinch of salt
· lemon juice (enough to make a thick icing/frosting)
· candied and glacé fruits
· edible flowers (optional)

Prinsesstarta ('princess cake')

This Swedish cake has fascinated me ever since I got the baking bug – you would expect 'princess cake' to be pink and elaborately decorated. Quite the contrary: this cake is covered in pastel-green marzipan with a dainty pink rose on top and very few piping details. It is usually dome-shaped but I have kept it flat as it's easier to portion and shape. I have taken the liberty of decorating it in my style but keeping the green and pink colours.

This cake is simple but it involves a few steps, so start early in the day or spread the steps out over several days. Marzipan with a high almond content (50–70%) will make all the difference.

---

1 Butter and line the base of a 20cm (8in) round cake tin with baking paper. Preheat the oven to 165°C fan/185°C/360°F/Gas mark 4½.

2 Sift the flour and salt into a large bowl.

3 In another large bowl if using a hand-held whisk, or a stand mixer with a whisk attachment, whisk the eggs, sugar and vanilla for 6–8 minutes until trebled in volume. Once fluffy and pale, gently fold in the sifted flour in 3–4 goes, combining after each addition.

4 Pour the melted butter gently into the whisked batter from the side of the bowl and fold in until no butter or flour streaks remain. Be careful not to deflate the air in the batter.

5 Pour the batter into the prepared tin. Tap the tin gently on the worktop to release any air pockets. Bake for 35–40 minutes, or until the surface is springy to touch and a skewer comes out clean.

6 Leave the cake to cool in the tin for 10 minutes, then turn out onto a cooling rack and remove the baking paper. Allow the cake to cool completely. Once cool, use a long serrated knife to cut it horizontally into 3 discs.

7 Wash and dry the tin ready for assembling the cake later. Line it with 2 sheets of cling film (plastic wrap), allowing a slight overhang.

8 To make the filling, whisk the double cream into soft peaks, then fold in the crème pâtissière.

Continued...

- 50g (3½ Tbsp) butter, melted, plus extra for greasing
- 150g (1 cup plus 2 Tbsp) self-raising flour
- ¼ tsp salt
- 5 large eggs
- 150g (¾ cup plus 1 Tbsp) golden caster (superfine) sugar
- ½ tsp vanilla bean paste

For the filling
- 500ml (1¾ cups plus 3 Tbsp) double (heavy) cream
- ½ batch of Crème Pâtissière (page 49)
- 150g (about ½ cup) raspberry jam (jelly)
- 100g (about 1 cup) fresh raspberries

To decorate
- 150g (about ½ cup) good-quality marzipan (rolled icing); I use 'Odense marcipan'
- 4 Tbsp pistachio paste
- cornflour (cornstarch) for dusting, optional
- 100g (3½oz) white chocolate, melted (page 19)
- 200g (2 cups) pistachios, finely chopped
- 50g (5 Tbsp) pistachio nibs
- edible flowers and leaves
- gold dust (optional)

Assembly

9 Place one of the cake discs in the base of the lined tin. Spread with a generous layer of raspberry jam. Scatter a few fresh raspberries over it. Then use half of the crème pâtissière to form a layer, then top with the second cake disc. Add the jam and raspberries as before and form another layer with the rest of the crème pâtissière. Place the third cake disc in the tin.

10 Place the cake in the freezer for 1 hour, or until it is solid.

11 Meanwhile, prepare the marzipan layer. Knead the marzipan and the pistachio paste together to a soft green, dough-like consistency. If it is sticking too much, dust with a little cornflour.

12 Roll out the marzipan to the thickness of a pound or dollar coin. Cut a 20cm (8in) diameter circle.

13 Ease the chilled cake out of the tin using the cling film to help. Use a hair dryer if it is stuck. Remove all the cling film and transfer the cake to a serving plate or a cake board.

14 Spread half of the melted chocolate on top of the cake and place the marzipan disc on top. Now spread the rest of the melted white chocolate on the side of the cake and cover the side of the cake with the finely chopped pistachios and pistachio nibs. The white chocolate will act as a glue for the pistachios.

15 Decorate the side of the cake with edible flowers and some leaves such as sweet cicely, mint and basil. Place a few pink flowers on top of the cake. Dust with gold (optional).

16 Keep the cake in the fridge until required. It is best eaten on the day it is made.

Tip You can colour the marzipan if you wish. I don't use artificial colouring but it is an option. Another option is to keep things simple and not use any colouring or pistachio paste at all.

Chai masala tres leches cake

Tres leches cakes are popular in Latin America: the 'three milks' – condensed milk, milk and cream – are poured all over the baked cake, giving it a pudding-like texture. It is an amazing make-ahead recipe and is very forgiving, even if the cake is slightly overbaked or dry.

The milky component reminds me of Indian desserts so I spice mine up with milky chai masala. Tea and cake have never been better: Indian flavours infused in a Mexican cake, with an extra crumble of 'biskoot'.

---

1 Butter and line a 20cm (8in) cake tin with a large sheet of baking paper with a slight overhang. Preheat the oven to 165°C fan/185°C/360°F/Gas mark 4½.

2 Sift the flour and salt into a large bowl and mix in the ground almonds and chai masala.

3 Mix the melted butter and vanilla in a small jug.

4 Put the eggs and sugar in a large bowl if using a hand-held whisk, or a stand mixer with a whisk attachment. Whisk until double in volume and fluffy and pale. Gently fold in the sifted flour in 3–4 goes, combining after each addition.

5 Pour the melted butter gently into the whisked batter from the side of the bowl and fold in until no butter or flour streaks remain. Be careful not to deflate the air in the batter.

6 Pour the batter into the prepared tin. Tap the tin gently on the worktop to release any air pockets. Bake for 35–40 minutes, or until a skewer comes out clean. Leave the cake in the tin to cool for 10–15 minutes.

7 While the cake is baking, make the chai masala milk. Put the milk, chai masala and black tea in a pan over a medium heat. Let it simmer for 5–7 minutes. Turn off the heat and leave it to cool and infuse for 20 minutes.

8 Strain and measure the milky tea. You should have about 200ml (¾ cup).

Continued…

- 25g (1 Tbsp plus 2 tsp) butter, melted, plus extra for greasing
- 150g (1 cup plus 2 Tbsp) plain (all-purpose) flour, plus extra for dusting
- ¼ tsp salt
- 100g (1 cup) ground almonds
- 1 Tbsp Chai Masala (page 201)
- ½ tsp vanilla bean paste
- 5 large eggs
- 150g (⅔ cup) golden caster (superfine) sugar

For the milk
- 300ml (1 cup plus 3 Tbsp) milk
- 2 Tbsp Chai Masala (page 201)
- 2 Tbsp black tea leaves or 3 teabags
- 150g (½ cup) condensed milk
- 250ml (1 cup) double (heavy) cream

For the topping
- 250ml (1 cup) double (heavy) cream
- 1 tsp sifted icing (confectioners') sugar

To decorate (optional)
- Chai Masala (page 201), for sprinkling
- 50g (1¾oz) biscuits of your choice, coarsely crumbled
- edible flowers

9 Wash the pan out. Add the prepared tea, condensed milk and double cream to the pan. Heat at a simmer for 2–3 minutes: it needs to be hot but not boiling.

10 Meanwhile, the cake will have cooled in its tin. Poke holes with a fork or skewer all over the surface.

11 Pour half the prepared milk mixture over the cake, reserving the other half for serving. Leave the cake to soak up the milk mixture for about an hour, at room temperature. Transfer the cake, still in the tin and covered slightly with cling film (plastic wrap), to the fridge for 6–8 hours, or overnight.

12 When ready to serve, remove the cake from the fridge and, gently lifting it out using the overhang, turn out of the tin onto a serving plate. If you want you can then trim off the excess paper and slightly neaten the edges, using a palette knife. I leave the paper for the rustic look.

13 To make the topping, whisk the double cream and icing sugar to soft peaks. Either spoon it all over the cake or use a piping bag fitted with a large star nozzle to pipe it on.

14 Sprinkle with chai masala and some biscuit crumbs, if you wish.

15 Serve, cut into wedges, with extra chai milk. Decorate with rose petals or pink flowers. These 2 colours look great together.

Tip

The chai masala powder can be prepared in advance and stored in a small airtight container for up to a month.

Austrian sachertorte

One of the most famous chocolate cakes in the world is the sachertorte – rich chocolate cake with a layer of apricot jam, encased in an indulgent chocolate coating. In Vienna is a hotel café where they claim the cake was invented. As soon as you sit down, you are transported to a different era. It has chandeliers and plush, burgundy-coloured velvet seats and curtains, and a wedge of cake is served with a generous helping of whipped cream. This is my version.

1 Butter and line the base and sides of a 20cm (8in) cake tin with baking paper. Preheat the oven 150°C fan/170°C/340°F/ Gas mark 3½.

2 Melt the chocolate in a glass or metal bowl over a pan of barely simmering water. Stir, then set aside.

3 Put the flour, baking powder, butter and salt in a large bowl and rub together to form a breadcrumb-like mixture.

4 In another large, very clean bowl, if using a hand-held mixer, or a stand mixer with a whisk attachment , whisk the egg whites to medium-firm peaks. Transfer to another large bowl and set aside.

5 Add the egg yolks to the empty bowl. Whisk for 2–3 minutes, add the sugar and whisk for a further 2–3 minutes, until the mixture is fluffy and pale: do not overmix. Add the flour and butter mixture, then fold in the melted chocolate and vanilla. Mix well until everything is combined. Gently fold in the meringue in 3–4 goes, using a large metal spoon or spatula.

6 Pour the batter into the prepared tin. Tap the tin gently on the worktop to release any air pockets. Bake for about 35–40 minutes, or until the surface is springy to touch and a skewer comes out clean.

7 Let the cake cool in the tin for 10–15 minutes, then turn out onto a wire rack to cool completely.

8 Once the cake has cooled, brush the top and sides of the cake with the warm jam. Leave at room temperature for about an hour. The coating of jam adds flavour and locks in the cake's moisture.

- 125g (½ cup plus 1 Tbsp) butter, plus extra for greasing
- 200g (7oz) dark chocolate (55% cocoa)
- 125g (1 cup minus 1 Tbsp) plain (all-purpose) flour
- 1 tsp baking powder
- ¼ tsp salt
- 5 eggs, separated
- 125g (⅔ cup) golden caster (superfine) sugar
- 1 tsp vanilla extract
- 4 Tbsp apricot jam (jelly), slightly warmed

For the chocolate glaze

- 150g (5½oz) dark chocolate (70% cocoa), finely chopped
- 175ml (½ cup plus 3 Tbsp) double (heavy) cream
- 1 Tbsp sunflower oil
- 1 Tbsp golden syrup (or dark corn syrup, honey, maple syrup or liquid glucose)

To decorate (optional)

- edible flowers
- gold dust

9 To make the chocolate glaze, put the chopped chocolate in a medium bowl. Pour the double cream into a small pan over a gentle heat and bring just to a simmer. Pour it over the chocolate. Leave for 5 minutes, then stir to a smooth, glossy ganache. Add the oil and syrup, and give it a final stir.

10 Pour the thick glaze over the jam-coated chocolate cake and leave to set completely.

11 Once set, decorate with edible flowers and gold dust, if you wish.

12 This cake keeps well at room temperature for 4–5 days. Serve a wedge with lots of whipped double cream, as they do in Vienna.

Moroccan m'hanncha

I adore Middle Eastern and North African desserts. This Moroccan cake is filled with a paste similar to frangipane, encased within crisp buttery filo pastry layers and an abundance of nuts, then drenched in spiced sugar syrups. What's not to like? M'hanncha is like one giant baklava: sticky, sweet and very moreish. Share, gathered around the table, with clotted cream and a drizzle of honey. It's a real crowd-pleaser.

---

1 Butter and flour a 20cm (8in) round cake tin. Line the base with a disc of baking paper. Preheat the oven to 180°C fan/200°C/400°F/Gas mark 6.

2 First prepare the frangipane. Put all the ingredients in a large bowl and mix together until well combined. Set aside.

3 M'hanncha is a coil-shaped pastry. We need to create a big long sausage with the filo. Take 10–12 filo pastry sheets and cut them in half lengthways. Keep them under a clean, damp tea towel (dish towel).

4 Place a second clean, damp tea towel on the work surface. Cut a large strip of baking paper, around 50cm x 50cm.

5 Lay out one cut sheet of filo pastry. Brush it with the ghee or melted butter. Now place a second sheet on top and brush again with the ghee or butter. Repeat with a third layer. Keep them under the tea towel.

6 Repeat this process to create three-layer sheets until you have used up all the filo. You will get between 6 and 9 strips of pastry.

7 Now place one of the pastry strips in front of you with a long side near you. Spoon a thin layer of the frangipane along its length and roll the filo into a tight cigar, encasing the frangipane. Coil it to a tight round shape. Place it on the centre of the sheet of baking paper. Cover with a dampened tea towel while you prepare the next coil.

8 Do the same with a second strip of pastry, filling it with a thin layer of frangipane and again rolling into a tight cigar. Wind this around the first coil, as tightly as you can. Repeat with another strip of filo and coil around the existing ones. This should make a coil about 20cm (8in) in diameter to fit snugly in the tin.

Continued...

- butter, for greasing
- flour, for dusting
- 250g (9oz) filo (phyllo) pastry (if using supermarket pastry, use 2 packs)
- 100g (½ cup minus 1 Tbsp) ghee or melted butter

For the frangipane

- 100g (½ cup minus 1 Tbsp) butter
- 200g (2 cups) ground almonds
- 100g (1 cup) ground pistachios (page 19)
- 100g (generous ½ cup) golden caster (superfine) sugar
- 2 eggs
- 25g (3 Tbsp) plain (all-purpose) flour
- ½ tsp salt
- 1 tsp rose water

For the syrup

- 300g (generous 1½ cups) golden caster (superfine) sugar
- 250ml (1 cup) water
- juice of ½ lemon (add the squeezed rind to the syrup too)
- ½ tsp salt
- 5–6 green cardamom pods, pods slightly cracked
- 10–12 saffron strands

To decorate

- pistachio nibs and dried rose petals

9 Lift the pastry coil with the baking paper into the prepared tin. Brush the coils generously with ghee. Repeat the same process with the remaining strips of filo to create a second coil and slide it over the existing coiled pastry in the tin. If you have any pastry or frangipane left over, you can use it up in a similar way. It does not need to be perfect. Brush with more ghee.

10 Bake for 40–45 minutes, or until it is a deep golden amber colour, the pastry is cooked through and golden and crisp.

11 While the cake is in the oven, make the syrup. Put all the ingredients except the saffron in a pan over a gentle heat and allow the sugar to melt. Gently simmer until it has a honey-like consistency. Remove from the heat. Let it cool slightly and add the saffron. The cardamom and saffron go well together here.

12 Take the m'hanncha out of the oven. While still warm, drizzle with the slightly cooled syrup. Leave it in the tin to cool.

13 Once slightly cooled, using the paper, lift out the m'hanncha and slide it onto a serving plate. Sprinkle with pistachios and rose petals. Serve with any remaining syrup and some clotted cream.

Dessert-inspired cakes

I love desserts as much as cakes. This chapter combines my love for both. Imagine panna-cotta-soaked sponges or delicate pancakes layered with mascarpone, mango ice cream or pistachio meringue, strawberry cheesecake or chocolate mousse.

All of these can take the form of a cake to bring something special to your table. And, if there is a birthday, put a candle on it.

Passion fruit and mango pancake cake

When running a business from home got lonely, I began looking for ways to connect with people. I came across a cookbook club, hosted by the ever-gracious and kind Thane Prince. I am lucky to have had her support and guidance ever since. The club was held in a lovely pub in Islington. We would all cook according to a theme. One meeting happened to fall on Shrove Tuesday so the theme was, of course, pancakes. There was an amazing selection of dishes, sweet and savoury, and my contribution was this cake.

I have used Indian mangoes but feel free to experiment with strawberries in summer or stone fruits and berries in autumn. Make it a day in advance to allow enough chilling time.

---

1 Sift the flour and salt into a large mixing bowl.

2 Put the eggs, milk and vanilla into a large jug or bowl. Tip in the flour and, using a balloon whisk, mix it to a smooth batter. The consistency should be thin, like single (light) cream.

3 Set aside a couple of spoonfuls of the butter and gently melt the rest in a small pan. Add the warm butter to the prepared pancake batter. Give it a stir and let it rest for 10 minutes.

4 Heat a 20cm (8in) frying pan (skillet). Brush it lightly with the remaining butter. Add a ladleful of the pancake batter and evenly coat the base of the pan to make a very thin pancake. It should only cook for under a minute or so on each side. Flip it out of the pan and keep on a plate.

5 Continue with the remaining batter to make approximately 25 pancakes (this will depend on the size of your ladle – don't worry if you make more!). Layer each pancake with a piece of baking paper as you go to prevent them sticking to one another.

6 To make the filling, put the mango purée, passion fruit purée and lime juice in a small pan. Add the cornflour paste to the mix. Gently heat for 5–7 minutes to cook the cornflour. Turn off the heat and leave the mixture to cool completely.

7 Put the mascarpone, double cream, icing sugar and lime zest in a large bowl and whisk until soft peaks form: do not overmix.

Continued…

- 350g (2⅔ cups) plain (all-purpose) flour
- ¼ tsp salt
- 5 eggs
- 600ml (2½ cups) milk
- 2 tsp vanilla bean paste
- 75g (⅓ cup) butter, plus extra for greasing

For the filling and topping

- flesh from 6 Indian mangoes (2 chopped into small pieces and 4 made into a purée)
- 100ml (7 Tbsp) passion fruit purée or juice from 6–7 passion fruits, seeds removed
- zest and juice of 2 limes
- 1 Tbsp cornflour (cornstarch) mixed with 2 Tbsp water
- 500g (2 cups plus 3 Tbsp) mascarpone
- 500ml (1¾ cups plus 3 Tbsp) double (heavy) cream
- 75g (½ cup plus 1 Tbsp) sifted icing (confectioners') sugar

To decorate (optional)

- pistachio nibs
- edible flower and petals

Assembly

8 Double-line a 20cm (8in) round cake tin with sides 7.5cm (3in) deep with cling film (plastic wrap), covering the sides and base, and leaving an overhang.

9 Set aside about a third of the mascarpone cream and 4 tablespoons of the fruit purée for decorating the cake later.

10 Put the first pancake in the base of the lined tin. Add a thin layer of the mascarpone cream, followed by a drizzle of the purée and a few pieces of the chopped mango. Repeat this layering process until all the pancakes, cream and purée have been used up.

11 Cover the top of the cake with cling film and place the tin in the fridge for 6–12 hours.

12 Once ready to serve, remove the cake from the fridge and discard the top layer of cling film. Carefully place a plate over the tin, and quickly invert the cake tin onto the plate so the top pancake becomes the base. Lift off the tin carefully and remove all remaining cling film.

13 Spread the reserved mascarpone cream on the top, and neaten the sides, if required.

14 Drizzle over the remaining fruit purée. Decorate with pistachio nibs and edible flowers. Serve chilled.

Basque cheesecake with berries

This rich, baked cheesecake has a dark burnt top and, unlike a traditional cheesecake, is made without a crust – which I prefer. This cake needs time, not so much in baking but in chilling in the fridge. This makes it a great bake-ahead dessert. It's well worth the patience. I like to serve it with seasonal berries and compôte.

1 Lightly butter and line the base and sides of a 20cm (8in) round cake tin with 2 sheets of baking paper, enough to come at least 8cm (3in) above sides of the tin. (This extra paper is required to lift the cheesecake once baked, and it helps the cheesecake rise during baking.) Preheat the oven to 220°C fan/240°C/475°F/Gas mark 9.

2 Put the cream cheese, soured cream, sugar, vanilla, salt and cornflour in a large bowl if using a hand-held beater, or a stand mixer with the paddle attachment and mix everything together.

3 Gently whisk the eggs and double cream together in a small jug or bowl using a balloon whisk or fork. With the machine running on low speed, slowly add the egg and cream mixture to the cream cheese mixture. Keep the speed low and stop when everything is well combined. Avoid overmixing, as this would create air bubbles in the cheesecake.

4 If you see any lumps, or unmixed mixture, you can pass this batter through a large metal sieve (strainer).

5 Pour the cheesecake into the prepared tin. Bake for 10 minutes, then reduce the temperature to 200°C fan/220°C/425°F/Gas mark 7 and bake for a further 40 minutes. You will know when it is done, as the top of the cheesecake will be dark and puffed up. It should still have a slight wobble in the middle, which is important for a creamy texture. Don't overbake the cheesecake. Do not be alarmed if it sinks a little.

6 Let it cool in the tin for an hour or two, then place in the fridge and leave overnight.

7 When ready to serve, use the baking paper to lift the cheesecake out of the tin. Decorate with some edible flowers, if you wish. Cut into wedges and serve with some berries or berry compôte on the side.

- butter, for greasing
- 550g (2½ cups plus 2 Tbsp) full-fat cream cheese
- 125g (½ cup) soured cream
- 150g (¾ cup plus 1 Tbsp) golden caster (superfine) sugar
- 1 tsp vanilla bean paste
- ½ tsp salt
- 40g (scant ½ cup) cornflour (cornstarch)
- 5 eggs
- 300ml (1 cup plus 3 Tbsp) double (heavy) cream

To serve (optional)
- fresh berries or berry compôte
- edible flowers

Saffron, pistachio and cardamom panna cotta cake with figs

Panna cotta is one of my favourite desserts. This make-ahead cake version can be served at dinner parties or used as a celebration cake. Here I have used fresh purple figs and ruby-red pomegranates but you can change the flavours with the season: berries or tropical fruits in summer and stone fruits later in the year.

1 Butter and line a 20cm (8in) round cake tin cake with baking paper. Preheat the oven to 165°C fan/185°C/360°F/ Gas mark 4½.

2 Sift the flour, baking powder, ground pistachios and salt into a large bowl.

3 Mix the melted butter and vanilla in a small jug.

4 Put the eggs and sugar in another large bowl if using a hand-held whisk, or a stand mixer with a whisk attachment. Whisk until the mixture has tripled in volume and is fluffy and pale. Gently fold in the dry ingredients in 2–3 goes, combining each addition so that no flour streaks remain.

5 Pour the melted butter into the batter from the side of the bowl and gently fold in until no butter streaks remain. Be careful not to deflate the batter.

6 Pour the batter into the prepared tin. Tap the tin gently on the worktop to release any air pockets. Bake for 35–40 minutes, or until the surface is springy to touch and a skewer comes out clean.

7 Leave the cake to cool in the tin for 10 minutes, then turn out onto a wire rack and remove the baking paper. Leave to cool completely while you make the rest. Wash and dry the tin ready for assembling the cake later.

8 To make the panna cotta, put the cream, milk, sugar and vanilla in a small pan over a gentle heat, then add the saffron strands and cardamom. Bring to a simmer.

9 Meanwhile, put the gelatine sheets in a small bowl with some water and leave to soak.

Continued…

- 25g (3 Tbsp) butter, melted, plus extra for greasing
- 150g (1 cup plus 2 Tbsp) plain (all-purpose) flour
- 1 tsp baking powder
- 100g (about 1 cup) ground pistachios (see page 19)
- ¼ tsp salt
- ½ tsp vanilla bean paste
- 4 large eggs
- 150g (¾ cup plus 1 Tbsp) golden caster (superfine) sugar

For the panna cotta
- 450ml (1¾ cups) double (heavy) cream
- 100ml (7 Tbsp) milk
- 50g (scant ¼ cup) golden caster (superfine) sugar
- ¼ tsp vanilla extract
- 4 sheets gelatine
- 15 saffron strands
- ¼ tsp ground cardamom

For the topping
- 250ml (1 cup) double (heavy) cream
- 15g (2 Tbsp) sifted icing (confectioners') sugar
- 10–12 saffron strands, lightly crushed
- 3 fresh figs
- 5 Tbsp honey

10 Once the gelatine sheets have swelled, squeeze out the water and add the sheets to the warm cream mixture. Turn off the heat, stir and leave to cool slightly.

Assembly

11 Double-line your tin with cling film (plastic wrap), covering the sides and the base, and allowing some overhang. Place the cake back in the lined tin and make large holes all over the surface using a chopstick or skewer. Pour half the lukewarm panna cotta mixture over the cake and leave to soak for 10 minutes, gently tapping the tin a few times to help it soak in. Pour the rest of the panna cotta over the soaked cake.

12 Cover the top of the cake with cling film and place the tin in the fridge for 6–12 hours.

13 Once ready to serve, prepare the topping. Whisk the double cream and icing sugar together in a bowl and swirl in the saffron. Quarter the figs and drizzle with honey.

14 Remove the cake from the fridge. Lift the chilled cake out of the tin with the help of the cling film. Remove all the cling film and place the cake on a serving plate or cake stand.

15 Top the cake with the saffron cream. Give it a few rustic swirls with the back of a small spoon. Arrange the honey-coated figs on top. Sprinkle with pomegranate kernels, pistachio nibs and edible flowers, if you wish.

To decorate (optional)
- pomegranate kernels
- pistachio nibs
- edible flowers

Chocolate mousse cake

In 2012, when I started my business, I catered for a huge 60th birthday party, creating an elaborate dessert table with frangipane tarts, pistachio macaroons, fig friands, tropical fruit cream tarts and this mousse cake. I still don't know how I did it all from my little home kitchen! The mousse cake became a favourite. You can make it ahead – perfect for special occasions and for days in between! The method is simple but time-consuming so don't attempt it on a day you are stretched.

Using a second 20cm (8in) springform or loose-bottomed tin to make the mousse helps with unmoulding, but you can wash and dry the first tin.

1 Butter and line a 20cm (8in) round cake tin cake with baking paper. Preheat the oven to 160°C fan/180°C/350°F/Gas mark 4.

2 Put the egg whites in a large, very clean bowl if using a hand-held whisk, or a stand mixer with a whisk attachment. Whisk for 5 minutes at a medium speed until the whites form stiff peaks when you lift the whisk. Set aside.

3 Put the yolks in a separate large bowl and whisk for 2–3 minutes at a medium speed then add the sugar and whisk until the mixture is fluffy, pale and almost doubled in volume. Put a few spoonfuls of the mixture in a bowl and mix in the sifted cocoa powder, then add the salt and vanilla extract. Use a spatula to gently fold the cocoa mixture back into the bowl of egg yolks and sugar.

4 Now gently fold the meringue into the chocolatey egg mixture in 3–4 goes, trying not to deflate the batter. Fold until everything is mixed well, scraping the base of the bowl too. Do not overmix.

5 Pour the batter into the prepared tin. Tap the tin gently on the worktop to release any air pockets. Bake for 25–30 minutes, or until a skewer comes out clean. Being flourless, it will look airy once baked but will deflate a little as it cools.

6 Leave the cake in the tin to cool completely, then turn out onto a wire rack and peel off the baking paper. Cut the cake horizontally into 2 discs (see page 34). Wrap in cling film (plastic wrap) and set aside.

7 Double-line the mousse tin (see intro) with cling film, covering the sides and base, leaving an overhang.

Continued..

- butter, for greasing
- 6 eggs, separated
- 120g (⅔ cup) golden caster (superfine) sugar
- 75g (¾ cup) sifted cocoa powder
- ¼ tsp salt
- 1 tsp vanilla extract
- 1 batch Chocolate Glaze (see page 51)

For the mousse
- 600ml (2¼ cups plus 2 Tbsp) double (heavy) cream
- 170g (6oz) dark chocolate (70% cocoa), finely chopped
- 170g (6oz) milk chocolate, finely chopped
- 100g (generous ½ cup) golden caster (superfine) sugar
- 1 Tbsp instant coffee dissolved in 80ml (⅓ cup) lukewarm water
- 3 egg yolks
- 1 tsp vanilla extract

To decorate
- edible flowers (optional)
- chocolate shavings

Tip
You can assemble the cake several days in advance, then cover with the glaze and any decorations on the day you serve it. Follow the recipe up to step 13, leaving the cake in the freezer for 3–4 days rather than overnight, then follow the rest of the steps as given.

8 Divide the double cream between 2 large bowls. Whip the cream in the first bowl to soft peaks. Put in the fridge to chill until required. Then heat the remaining cream to a gentle simmer. Put the chocolate in a medium bowl and pour the heated cream over the chocolate. Leave for 5–6 minutes, then stir to form a glossy ganache. Set aside.

9 In another small pan, mix the sugar and coffee mixture together and simmer over a medium heat for 6–8 minutes: the sugar will melt and turn a light golden colour.

10 Meanwhile, put the egg yolks and vanilla into a clean bowl or the stand mixer and whisk at a medium speed until pale and thick. Carefully pour in the hot sugar syrup in a thin stream. Immediately whisk at a medium to high speed until it has doubled in volume and is fluffy and pale.

11 Fold the ganache into the egg yolk mixture in 2–3 goes and let it cool for 5 minutes. Finally, take the whipped cream from the fridge and fold it into the chocolate and egg mixture in 3–4 goes, folding carefully after each addition.

Assembly

12 Pour half of the chocolate mousse mixture into your lined cake tin. Place one of the chocolate cake discs over the mousse. Press it down gently. Pour over the rest of the mousse, then top with the second cake disc. Give the top cake layer a gentle press so that mousse comes up the sides.

13 Cover the cake with cling film and place the tin in the freezer for at least 8 hours, or overnight.

14 Six hours before you plan to serve the cake, take the cake out of the freezer. To unmould it, use a hair dryer on a medium setting. Direct it at the base and sides of the tin for a couple of minutes, then use the cling film to ease the cake from the tin. Remove all the cling film and place a plate or cake board on top of the tin, then invert the cake so that the top cake layer becomes the base.

15 Meanwhile, make the chocolate glaze following the method on page 51.

16 Place the still-frozen cake on a wire rack with a tray underneath. Pour over the slightly warm chocolate glaze so it covers the top and sides of the cake. As the cake is frozen, it will set quickly. Sprinkle with edible flowers, if you like, and cut using a sharp, clean knife.

17 Keep refrigerated for up to 3 days.

Pistachio meringue, rose and rhubarb cake

This cake is somewhere in between soft squishy pavlova and crisp meringue and uses some of my favourite ingredients – pistachio, rose water, meringue and rhubarb. This meringue is baked in a tin to give a more structured look – it certainly holds better for garden parties! You could use hazelnuts and berries instead, if you like.

1 Lightly grease 2 shallow 20cm (8in) cake tins with sunflower oil and line the bases with baking paper. Preheat the oven to 160°C fan/180°C/350°F/Gas mark 4.

2 Line a baking tray with baking paper. Spread out the sugar in a single layer. Place in the preheated oven for 10 minutes.

3 Meanwhile, put the egg whites in a large, very clean bowl if using a hand-held whisk, or a stand mixer with a whisk attachment. Whisk until stiff peaks form.

4 Take the sugar out of the oven and reduce the temperature to 110°C fan/130°C/260°F/Gas mark ¾.

5 Add spoonfuls of the warm sugar to the egg whites, continuously whisking after each addition at a medium speed. Add all the sugar this way and whisk for a further 7–8 minutes at a high speed to form a thick and glossy meringue.

6 Carefully and quickly fold in the remaining meringue ingredients using a large metal spoon. Try not to deflate it. Then divide the meringue between the tins. Spread evenly with the back of the spoon.

7 Place in the oven for about 1 hour and 15 minutes. Once baked, switch off the oven and leave the meringue inside for a couple of hours, with the oven door slightly ajar.

8 Carefully remove the meringue from the tins and remove the paper. It is ready to be assembled.

Assembly

9 To make the filling, put the cream, mascarpone and vanilla in a bowl and whip until soft peaks form.

10 Place one of the meringue layers on a serving plate. Dollop over the whipped cream. Generously spoon over the rhubarb compôte and top it with the second meringue layer. Finish by sprinkle with pistachio nibs and edible flowers, if you wish.

11 This can be stored for up to 3 hours in the fridge. It's best eaten on the day it's assembled.

- sunflower oil, for greasing
- 185g (1 cup) golden caster (superfine) sugar
- 4 large egg whites
- 150g (1½ cups) pistachios, coarsely ground or very finely chopped
- ¼ tsp salt
- ½ tsp vanilla extract
- ¼ tsp rose water

For the filling

- 350ml (1¼ cups plus 2 Tbsp) double (heavy) cream
- 250g (1 cup plus 1 Tbsp) mascarpone
- 1 tsp vanilla bean extract
- rhubarb compôte, prepared according to the instructions on page 47

To decorate (optional)

- handful of pistachio nibs
- edible flowers

Rose, cardamom and pistachio custard cake

There is an Indian regional sweet called khaaja. In Hindi, it literally means 'eat it'. The texture is light, flaky and airy – a miracle, considering it's a deep-fried filo pastry with a sugar syrup crust. Growing up, marriages and celebrations were incomplete without huge bamboo baskets of khaaja. It also made a breakfast of dreams, dunked in hot creamy milk.

When I first moved to London, my then-neighbour Zahra invited me round. Sitting at the dining table was her mother-in-law, carefully creating an Egyptian dessert called Umm ali. When we ate the delicious dish, I felt it was familiar and yet completely foreign. I walked home trying to figure out what it reminded me of. Then it struck me: it had the flavour of khaaja with hot milk. A few days later I asked Aunty to share her recipe. With my neighbour translating, Aunty's adorable hand movements and lots of laughter later, I managed to scribble something down. That day I learnt how food connects us deeply: it is a language in itself.

I lost touch with Zahra when we both moved homes, but that recipe stayed with me. Over the years, it has combined with my memories of khaaja: it now has the texture of Umm ali, but a flaky, crisp pastry top, like khaaja. This is egg-free, for my mother, but you can use a thin custard with eggs if you prefer.

---

1 Preheat the oven to 170°C fan/190°C/375°F/Gas mark 5.

2 Butter a 20cm (8in) round cake tin or use a springform cake tin. Line with a large piece of baking paper, pressing it well into the base and sides, and allowing a 2–3cm (a good inch) overhang.

3 Filo pastry dries very quickly so you have to work fast. Slightly dampen a clean tea towel (dish towel) and clear space on your counter. Unwrap the pastry and keep it covered under the damp tea towel.

4 Spread one sheet of the filo pastry and brush it all over with ghee. Sparingly sprinkle a teaspoon of the chopped pistachio and cashew nuts over the buttered filo. Keeping the sheet on the counter, gather it up lengthways in concertina folds. You will have a long thin strip of pastry with folds. Then fold in one short end of the strip and roll it into a rough rose or coil shape. Place in the lined cake tin. Repeat using the rest of the sheets and tuck all the coils snugly into the tin.

5 Brush the top with more ghee and bake in the oven for 18–20 minutes. The pastry should be amber golden and crisp, not pale and underbaked.

Continued..

- 100g (½ cup) ghee or butter, melted, plus extra for greasing
- 12 sheets filo pastry (generally 1 packet)
- 50g (about ½ cup) very finely chopped pistachio nuts
- 50g (about ½ cup) very finely chopped cashew nuts
- 150g (½ cup) condensed milk
- 250ml (1 cup) milk
- 250ml (1 cup) double (heavy) cream
- 3 Tbsp custard powder (instant vanilla pudding)
- 1 tsp vanilla bean paste
- 10–12 saffron strands
- ½ tsp ground cardamom

6 Take the tin out of the oven and reduce the temperature to 140°C fan/160°C/325°F/Gas mark 3.

7 Put the condensed milk, whole milk, cream, custard powder, vanilla, saffron and cardamom in a jug. Mix well using a fork or balloon whisk.

8 Pour the mixture over the baked filo coils and place the tin back in the oven for 20–25 minutes. The custard should be baked through and almost set, and the top should be crunchy and golden.

9 Remove from the oven and sprinkle with rose petals, pistachio nibs and cashew nuts, and drizzle honey over the top.

10 Once cooled to room temperature, have a large serving plate ready and carefully lift out the cake out using the overhang and place on the serving plate. You can snip off the sides of the paper using scissors if you like, but I take it to the table as it is.

11 The best way to serve it is using a large metal knife and a large metal spoon. Enjoy it at room temperature with pouring cream.

To decorate and serve
- rose petals, dried or fresh
- 2 Tbsp pistachio nibs
- 4 Tbsp orange blossom honey or any good-quality honey

Coconut, lime and pineapple tiramisu cake

There is something about the freshness of lime, pineapple, coconut and mint that screams tropical seaside holiday. When summer is here, bake this cake. It can be made the day before so call your friends over and enjoy this sitting in the sun. Place a retro cocktail umbrella on each serving, if you like. The rum is optional.

---

1 Butter or oil and line a 20cm (8in) round cake tin with baking paper. Preheat the oven to 165°C fan/185°C/360°F/ Gas mark 4½.

2 Sift the flour and salt into a large bowl, mix in the desiccated coconut and set aside.

3 Put the eggs and sugar in a large bowl if using a hand-held whisk, or a stand mixer with a whisk attachment. Whisk until tripled in volume and fluffy and pale, then gently fold in the dry ingredients until no flour streaks remain.

4 Pour in the melted butter and vanilla from the side of the bowl and fold in until no butter streaks remain. Be careful not to deflate the batter.

5 Pour the batter into the prepared tin. Tap the tin gently on the worktop to release any air pockets. Bake for 35–40 minutes, or until the surface is springy to touch and a skewer comes out clean.

6 Leave the cake to cool in the tin for 10 minutes, then turn out onto a wire rack and remove the baking paper. Leave to cool completely.

7 Carefully slice horizontally into 4 thin discs using a long serrated knife. Keep them covered until required.

8 Wash and dry the tin ready for assembling the cake later.

Continued...

- 45g (3 Tbsp) butter, melted, or sunflower oil, plus extra for greasing
- 150g (1 cup plus 2 Tbsp) self-raising flour
- ¼ tsp salt
- 100g (about 1½ cups) desiccated (shredded) coconut
- 5 large eggs
- 150g (¾ cup plus 1 Tbsp) golden caster (superfine) sugar
- ½ tsp vanilla bean paste

For the syrup

- 150ml (5fl oz) fresh pineapple juice (or use the juice from a can, if using, and make up the difference with water)
- 50g (scant ¼ cup) caster (superfine) sugar
- zest and juice of 2 limes
- 20 fresh mint leaves
- 25ml (1 Tbsp plus 2 tsp) white rum (optional)

For the pineapple filling

- 500g (1lb 2oz) peeled and trimmed fresh pineapple or approximately 450g (1lb) drained canned pineapple
- ½ tsp salt
- zest and juice of 1 lime

9 While the cake is baking, make the syrup. Put the pineapple juice (or juice and water), sugar, lime juice, and rum, if using, in a medium pan. Bring to a simmer over a medium heat until all the sugar has dissolved. Turn off the heat and add the lime zest and mint leaves. Leave for 1 hour to infuse and cool. Once cooled, strain the syrup, discarding the leaves, and set aside.

10 For the pineapple filling, chop the pineapple into small pieces and slightly crush them. Put in a bowl with the salt, lime zest and juice. Give everything a mix and set aside.

11 Put all the filling ingredients into a large bowl and whip until soft peaks form. Set aside.

Assembly

12 Double-line your tin, or use a springform tin, with cling film (plastic wrap), covering the base and sides well and leaving an overhang of at least 2cm (¾in).

13 Place one of the cake discs in the base of the lined cake tin. Brush the cake generously with the cooled syrup. Add a quarter of the cream filling. Spread it with the back of a spoon. Add a few spoonfuls of crushed pineapple on top. Place the second cake disc in the tin and repeat with the layering of syrup, filling and crushed pineapple, until all four cake discs are used, finishing with a layer of cream filling on top.

14 Cover lightly with cling film and chill in the fridge for at least 8 hours or overnight.

15 A few hours before serving, remove the cake from the fridge. Have a suitable cake stand and plate ready. Remove the top layer of the cling film and place the plate on the tin. Turn the cake out onto the plate. Carefully pull away the tin. Properly chilled cake is important here. Remove all the cling film from the sides and base of the cake. Tidy the sides using a cake palette knife if necessary.

16 Decorate with pineapple flowers, coconut chips, lime slices, mint sprigs, edible flowers and paper cocktail umbrellas, if you like.

For the filling

- 600ml (2¼ cups plus 2 Tbsp) double (heavy) cream
- 50g (6¾ Tbsp) sifted icing (confectioners' sugar)
- 160g (½ cup) coconut cream
- 500g (2 cups plus 3 Tbsp) mascarpone
- 1 tsp vanilla bean paste
- zest and juice of 1 lime

To decorate (optional)

- dried pineapple flowers (see page 197)
- coconut chips (flakes)
- lime slices
- mint sprigs
- edible flowers

Fruit and nut fridge cake

Growing up, for me, Cadbury's Dairy Milk Fruit & Nut was the ultimate chocolate bar. We did not have access to many foreign brands in India, except when relatives from abroad would visit. I used to save my pocket money to buy Fruit & Nut chocolate. During the summer, chocolate would melt quickly due to the intense heat so we would keep it in the fridge. Sometimes we would sandwich the melted chocolate between 2 Parle-G biscuits – similar to malted milks – to make a chocolate biscuit, for ease of eating.

Many years later, at a friend's child's birthday party, there was a chocolate fridge cake, cut into small pieces, on the table. I have met many people who have mentioned that a fridge cake was part of their childhood. For me, though, it is a memory of melted chocolate, biscuits and a Cadbury Fruit & Nut bar. This cake is a grown-up version of a childhood treat.

---

1 Line a 20cm (8in) round cake tin with a large piece of baking paper, covering the base and sides, and allowing a slight overhang.

2 Place the chocolate, butter and golden syrup in a heatproof bowl over a pan of barely simmering water. Let it melt.

3 Meanwhile, coarsely chop the biscuits.

4 Once the chocolate mixture has melted, stir in the nuts, biscuits and cranberries.

5 Pour the mixture into the prepared tin. Smooth it with the back of a spoon.

6 Place in the fridge to set for 2–3 hours.

7 Once completely set, lift the cake out of the tin using the baking paper.

8 To serve, cut into thin wedges and enjoy!

- 200g (7oz) dark chocolate (70% cocoa), broken into pieces
- 400g (14oz) milk chocolate, broken into pieces
- 200g (1 cup) butter, plus extra for greasing
- 5 Tbsp golden syrup (dark corn syrup)
- 200g (7oz) biscuits (ginger nuts, Rich Tea biscuits, wafers, graham crackers)
- 100g (about 1 cup) pistachios
- 50g (scant ½ cup) toasted almonds
- 100g (about 1 cup) dried cranberries

Strawberry cheesecake

I had my first strawberry when I was almost 25, the summer I moved to the UK. The flavour is still locked in my memory. I now eagerly look forward to visiting a pick-your-own strawberry farm once a year.

I believe this is one of the best summer desserts, with its pink colour, strawberry sweetness and biscuit–pistachio base, best served with fresh whipped cream and more delicious strawberries. A perfect make-ahead dessert for summer entertaining. Outside of summer, use other seasonal fruits like mangoes, blackberries or peaches.

This recipe calls for a double batch of crumbly base – the extra crumbs are served with the cheesecake for extra crunch and texture. I prefer a crisp, crunchy base so I recommend making biscuit crumbs from scratch, but you can use bought shortbread instead (see tip).

1 First make the crumb base as it needs to chill. Put all the ingredients into a large bowl and mix until it clumps together. Do not overmix: you want a coarse, rubble-like texture. Put it in a freezer-safe bag and freeze for 1 hour.

2 Preheat the oven to 160°C fan/180°C/350°F/Gas mark 4.

3 Line a baking tray with baking paper. Spread the crumble mixture across the tray. Bake for 12–15 minutes until lightly toasted, like large crumbs of a cookie.

4 Leave to cool completely on the tray. This can be prepared a couple of days in advance and stored in an airtight container.

5 Double-line a 20cm (8in) round cake tin, or use a springform cake tin, with cling film (plastic wrap).

6 Pack half the crumble mix into the base of the lined tin to form a firm layer. Save the rest for later.

7 To make the strawberry purée, chop the strawberries, place in a large bowl and sprinkle with caster sugar. Leave to macerate for 30 minutes.

8 Then, using a blender or food processor, purée the strawberries and pass through a fine sieve (strainer) into a small pan. Place over a very gentle heat.

9 Stir in the lemon juice and cornflour paste. Simmer for 3–4 minutes, stirring continuously, to cook the cornflour and slightly thicken the purée. Do not overcook: you want to preserve the freshness of the strawberries.

For the crumb base

- 150g (1 cup plus 2 Tbsp) plain (all-purpose) flour
- 85g (½ cup) caster (superfine) sugar
- 125g (½ cup plus 1 Tbsp) butter
- 100g (about 1 cup) pistachios, chopped
- 30g (2½ Tbsp) demerara (raw brown) sugar
- 1 tsp vanilla extract
- 1 Tbsp sea salt flakes

Tip

If you don't want to make the biscuit crumble layer, use 200g (½ cup) of good-quality, shop-bought shortbread and add 50g (7oz) chopped pistachios.

For the strawberry purée

- 200g (about 2 cups) strawberries, stems removed
- 30g (2 Tbsp) golden caster (superfine) sugar
- 1 Tbsp lemon juice
- 1 tsp cornflour (cornstarch) mixed with 2 Tbsp water

For the cheesecake layer

- 250ml (1 cup) double (heavy) cream
- 500g (2 cups plus 3 Tbsp) full-fat cream cheese
- 75g (½ cup plus 1 Tbsp) sifted icing (confectioners') sugar
- 125g (½ cup) soured cream
- 1 tsp vanilla extract
- ½ tsp salt
- 30g (2 tsp) freeze-dried strawberry powder (optional)

To finish

- 250ml (1 cup) double (heavy) cream (optional)
- 1 Tbsp icing (confectioners') sugar
- ½ tsp vanilla bean paste
- 250g (about 2½ cups) strawberries, quartered
- edible flowers and leaves
- 50g (about ½ cup) chopped green pistachios or pistachio nibs

10 Leave the purée to cool completely, then put it in the fridge for 1–2 hours. (This could be prepared a day ahead and stored in the fridge.)

11 Once the purée has chilled, make the cheesecake layer. Put the cream in a large bowl if using a hand-held whisk, or a stand mixer with a whisk attachment, and whip to soft peaks.

12 Scrape the cream into another bowl and use the same bowl and whisk the cream cheese, icing sugar, soured cream, vanilla and salt for a minute or two until everything is combined.

13 Add the strawberry purée and sift in the freeze-dried strawberry powder (if using). Fold gently to combine. Now gently fold in the whipped cream in 2–3 goes, using a spatula or a large metal spoon.

14 Spoon the mixture onto the crumb base in the tin. Give the tin a gentle tap to settle the mixture and place the tin in the fridge for at least 8 hours, or ideally overnight.

15 Once the cheesecake has set, ease it out of the tin with the help of the cling film. Place on a plate and remove the cling film.

16 To decorate the cheesecake, whip the cream (if using) with the icing sugar and vanilla. Spoon over the set cheesecake. Top it with quartered strawberries, and sprinkle with edible flowers, leaves such as mint, basil and/or sweet cicely, and pistachios.

Peach melba ice cream cake

For a man who has spent his life in a small town in India, Papa is remarkably aware of the world. I guess he is well-travelled through his books. He is always eager to learn, and he remembers everything! In the late '80s and '90s he subscribed to the food magazine Cuisine. *One issue had a Peach Melba: I remember being mesmerised by the vibrant photo and, to my amazement, Papa knew how it got its name. Back then, we didn't know what raspberries or peaches even looked like, but we had vanilla ice cream, one of the components of the dessert. So, sitting on the steps of the veranda, we ate vanilla ice cream with wafer biscuits, dreaming of eating Peach Melba one day.*

This cake is my re-imagining of how I had thought it would taste all those years ago. Technically this is not a cake, just layers assembled, but this book would be incomplete without it. Papa, this one's for you. Thank you for opening up the world for us and nurturing our dreams.

1 Double-line a 20cm (8in) round cake tin or a springform cake tin with cling film (plastic wrap), allowing an overhang.

2 To prepare the peaches, half-fill a large pan with water and bring to a gentle simmer.

3 Half-fill the largest bowl you have with ice and cold water.

4 Make a cross cut at the base of each peach. Gently lower the peaches into the simmering water. After 1 minute use a slotted spoon to transfer the peaches to the ice bath, one at a time. Gently peel off the skins. They should come off easily but a small knife will remove any remaining bits.

5 Halve the peaches and remove the stones. Take 2 peaches and slice them both into 6 wedges. Cover and put in the fridge. Chop the remaining 4 peaches into small pieces. Use a blender or food processor to reduce them to a smooth purée. Taste: if the peaches are not very sweet, you can add extra sugar.

6 Put the purée in a medium pan over a gentle heat and bring to a simmer. Add the cornflour paste and cook, stirring continuously, over a low heat for 5 minutes. Turn off the heat and leave to cool completely. The purée should be thick enough to coat the back of a spoon.

7 To make the raspberry purée, put 200g (about 1½ cups) of the raspberries in a large bowl and stir in the sugar. Cover the bowl with a clean tea (dish) towel and leave to macerate for 2–3 hours, then push the raspberries though a fine sieve (strainer) over another bowl, discarding the seeds caught

- 6 yellow flesh peaches
- 50g (scant ¼ cup) golden caster (superfine) sugar, plus extra, if needed, for the peaches
- 1 Tbsp cornflour (cornstarch) mixed with 2 Tbsp cold water
- 400g (about 3 cups) fresh raspberries
- 2 Tbsp lemon juice
- 2 x 500g (17fl oz) tubs of vanilla ice cream
- 180g (6oz) wafer biscuits, coarsely crushed

To decorate

- 150g (about 2 cups) almond flakes, lightly toasted
- 100g (3½oz) wafer biscuits
- edible flowers (optional)

in the sieve. Add the lemon juice to the raspberry purée, stir and set aside. Keep the remaining whole raspberries in the fridge until required.

8 Scoop 500g (17fl oz) of the vanilla ice cream into a bowl. Leave to soften slightly, but not melt. Once it has softened, add half the raspberry purée in dollops, swirling it with a skewer to create a ripple effect. Do not overmix.

Assembly

9 Spread 60g (2¼oz) of the wafer biscuits in a thin layer over the base of the prepared tin. Spoon the vanilla and raspberry ripple ice cream over the wafer layer and spread it evenly, levelling it with the back of a spoon. Place the tin in the freezer for 15 minutes to set it slightly.

10 Meanwhile, scoop the remaining 500g (17fl oz) of the vanilla ice cream into a bowl. Let it soften as before, then dollop half the peach purée into the ice cream and give it a swirl with a skewer to create a ripple effect.

11 Take the cake tin out of the freezer and add the vanilla and peach ripple ice cream to the tin, spreading it evenly with the back of a spoon.

12 Sprinkle another 60g (2¼oz) layer of wafer onto the ice cream.

13 Wrap the tin well with cling film (plastic wrap) and return it to the freezer for 6–8 hours, or until frozen.

14 When ready to serve, remove the tin from the freezer and remove the cling film. Invert the tin upside down on a large serving plate. If the cake is stuck, you can use a hair dryer on a medium setting to loosen the ice cream, or dip the tin briefly in a large bowl of hot water. It should then turn out easily.

15 Neaten the edges and press the remaining crushed wafer biscuits and some almond flakes onto the sides and top of the cake.

16 Top with the reserved sliced peaches and fresh raspberries. Drizzle with the remaining raspberry purée and more almond flakes. Sprinkle with edible flowers, if you wish.

17 To serve, cut into wedges and add some the remaining peach purée and wafer biscuits.

Tip

Wafer biscuits are thin, buttery and really crisp. If you cannot find any, use waffle ice cream cones instead.

Butterscotch cake

My husband and I were introduced by our parents and extended family. He grew up in the UK and I was from a small town in India. Even though our families knew of each other, there had been years of distance. If our very different worlds were to merge, we needed time to get to know one another.

We really liked each other but we were poles apart in temperament. So I wanted to know about the small, simple everyday things. For instance, I had to test whether he would get my crazy love for ice cream. Instead of a fancy restaurant, I arranged our first meeting alone by a local ice-cream cart in Delhi. We met in June, when temperatures peak: I still don't know if it was the heat or if he genuinely likes ice cream as much as I do, but we both had seconds that day, both ordering butterscotch ice cream each time. I gave him full marks and we got engaged the very next day. Our life together began with butterscotch ice cream and now, every year on 26th June, we celebrate with two bowlfuls. This is our 23rd year of marriage. When I started baking, I created this butterscotch cake, which tastes just like that special ice cream.

---

1 First make the praline. Preheat the oven to 150°C fan/170°C/340°F/Gas mark 3½. Line a baking tray with baking paper. Spread the pecans and almonds on the tray in a single layer and roast for 8–10 minutes until slightly toasted. Set aside to cool.

2 Put the sugar in a medium pan and cook over a low to medium heat. The sugar will melt and become a golden amber caramel: this can take up to 12–15 minutes. Once the sugar is the required colour, very carefully pour the hot caramel over the toasted nuts. Allow to cool and set completely.

3 Once the nuts are cold and set hard, use a rolling pin to bash the praline into pieces. Add the sea salt, then blitz in a food processor to make fine crumbs. Store the praline for up to 2 days.

4 To make the cake, butter and flour two 20cm (8in) round cake tins and line the bases with discs of baking paper.

5 Preheat the oven to 160°C fan/180°C/350°F/Gas mark 4.

6 Sift the flour, baking powder and salt into a large bowl.

Continued...

- butter, for greasing
- 250g (1¾ cups plus 2 Tbsp) plain (all-purpose) flour, plus extra for dusting
- 1½ tsp baking powder
- ½ tsp salt
- 240g (1 cup plus 1 Tbsp) Brown Butter (page 46), from 300g (1⅓ cups) butter, cooled to room temperature
- 125g (½ cup plus 2 Tbsp) golden caster (superfine) sugar
- 125g (½ cup plus 1 Tbsp) light soft brown sugar
- 1 tsp vanilla bean paste
- 4 eggs
- 60ml (4 Tbsp) milk or almond milk
- 75g (2¾oz) Pecan and Almond Praline (see below)

Pecan and almond praline

- 100g (about 1½ cups) pecan halves
- 100g (1 cup plus 2 Tbsp) whole, unskinned almonds
- 300g (1½ cups) golden caster (superfine) sugar
- 1 Tbsp salt

7 Put the soft brown butter in a large mixing bowl if using a hand-held beater, or a stand mixer with a beater attachment. Add both sugars and the vanilla and beat on a medium speed for 4–5 minutes until pale and fluffy. Add the eggs, one at a time, beating after each addition. Then sift in the flour mixture in 3 goes, folding after each addition. Add the milk and the pecan and almond praline crumbs and stir once more until just combined.

8 Divide the batter between the prepared tins and tap the tins gently on the worktop to release any air pockets. Bake for 25–30 minutes. Once baked, let the cakes cool in the tins for 10 minutes and then turn out onto wire racks.

9 Once slightly cooled, wrap the cakes in cling film (plastic wrap) and chill in the freezer for an hour.

10 To make the filling, whip the cream using a whisk attachment for 3–4 minutes on medium speed. Add the mascarpone, icing sugar and vanilla, and whisk until soft peaks form. Take care not to overbeat the mixture or it will curdle. Then switch to folding by hand using a spatula, to avoid overbeating. Cover and chill in the fridge for 30 minutes.

Assembly

11 Take the cakes from the freezer and unwrap. Cut each cake horizontally into 3 discs (see page 34): you will have 6 in total.

12 Mix together the milk or almond milk and vanilla.

13 Take the cream filling out of the fridge and spoon a quarter into another bowl for covering and finishing the cake. Return this bowl to the fridge.

14 Put a spoonful of the cream on a 25cm (10in) cake board or flat plate to help secure the cake. Place the first disc of the cake on top, then brush it all over with the prepared vanilla milk. Spread 2 large tablespoonfuls of the cream filling evenly over the cake, then sprinkle with a handful of the praline. Repeat with the next cake disc, cream and praline until everything is used up, finishing with a sponge layer on top.

Continued...

For the filling

· 400ml (1½ cups plus 3 Tbsp) double (heavy) cream
· 250g (1 cup plus 1 Tbsp) mascarpone
· 50g (6¾ Tbsp) icing (confectioners') sugar
· 1 Tbsp vanilla bean paste
· 100g (3½oz) Pecan and Almond Praline (see page 164)

For brushing the cake

· 100ml (7 Tbsp) milk or almond milk
· 1 tsp vanilla bean paste

To decorate

· 100g (3½oz) Pecan and Almond Praline (see page 164)
· edible flowers (optional)

To serve (optional)

· cream or ice cream

15 Cover the surface and sides of the cake with the reserved cream filling – a palette knife or a cake scraper dipped in lukewarm water is handy to neaten the sides.

16 Chill the cake for 30 minutes.

17 Once the cake has chilled, fully coat the sides and top with praline crumbs using your hand or the cake scraper, gently pressing in the praline.

18 Keep the cake chilled until required. It can be covered lightly with cling film and stored in the fridge for 2 days.

19 When ready to serve, decorate with edible flowers and more praline, if there are any leftovers, for added crunch, and serve with lots of cream or ice cream, if you wish.

Tips

· If you have only one tin, bake half the batter for 25–30 minutes, or until a skewer inserted into the cake comes out clean, then cool the cake for 10 minutes in the tin before turning out onto a wire rack. Wipe the tin with a clean cloth or paper towel, and prepare it again with butter, flour and baking paper. Bake the second half of the batter as per the first batch.

· If the layers slide during assembly, place the unfinished layer in the fridge to cool and set. Chilled cakes are easier to assemble.

· A couple of long, flat bamboo skewers or thick bubble tea straws can also be inserted through the layers of the cake to stop them sliding and to keep the layers in place. The straws can be left in and snipped level with the top the cake using sharp scissors. Remove before portioning and serving the cake.

Free-from cakes

A cake should be enjoyed by everyone, but sometimes dietary restrictions get in the way. For me, when baking a cake with special dietary restrictions it should appeal to all. There is no point making a cake that tastes like cardboard – it's not fair! For me, 'free-from' means inclusive cakes that everybody can enjoy, without anyone feeling that they are missing out. I am a home baker and rely on the usual flour, butter, eggs and sugar. However, I have received many requests for free-from cakes over the years, most commonly for gluten-free, egg-free and vegan cakes.

So here are eight recipes that can be baked keeping those three dietary restrictions in mind. No one will be able to tell the difference: they are equally delicious.

The recipes in this chapter are versatile and adaptable. For instance, the vegan chocolate cake is equally good on its own if you don't want to make a buttercream cake. You can also try the blueberry and plum cake warm as a pudding, served with custard.

Finally, for my Indian diaspora looking for an egg-free cake, please try the berries and fresh cream cake.

Egg-free date cake

This cake is based on a recipe I was given by a customer during my cake stall days. She very kindly said that my parents must love my baking. I said I was not sure: my mother does not eat eggs and I don't bake much without eggs. To my surprise, she shared a recipe for an old-fashioned, egg-free cake. The original only had soft dates and prunes but I have added other fruits.

Over the years, I have adapted it to my Ma's liking: it has her seal of approval. It keeps well and no one would guess it is 'free-from'. Enjoy it with strong tea with or pack it for picnics or long journeys – it keeps really well.

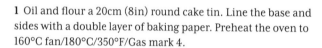

1 Oil and flour a 20cm (8in) round cake tin. Line the base and sides with a double layer of baking paper. Preheat the oven to 160°C fan/180°C/350°F/Gas mark 4.

2 Chop the dates, figs, prunes and apricots into small pieces. Put in a large bowl along with the currants. Add the orange zest and juice and leave to soak overnight, or for at least 6 hours until the fruits have become plump and soaked up all the liquid.

3 Put the butter, condensed milk, tea and all the soaked fruits in a medium pan over a very gentle heat and simmer for 5 minutes, stirring continuously. Turn off the heat and leave to cool for 10 minutes.

4 Sift both flours, the baking powder, bicarbonate of soda and salt into another large bowl. Pour in the warm fruit mixture and fold it well using a spatula.

5 Pour the batter into the prepared tin and level it with the back of a spoon. Tap the tin gently on the worktop to release any air pockets.

6 Bake for 1 hour, or until a skewer comes out clean, the cake is well-risen and springy to touch. After 30 minutes, cover the cake with a piece of foil if it is browning too much.

7 Leave the cake in the tin for 10 minutes, then turn it out onto a wire rack.

8 Once slightly cooled, brush the cake all over with the apricot glaze. Leave to set for a few hours. The texture of the cake improves as it matures over the next few days. Store it in an airtight container for a week, or wrap well and put in the freezer for a few months.

- oil, for greasing
- 125g (1 cup minus 1 Tbsp) plain (all-purpose) flour, plus extra for dusting
- 200g (about 1⅓ cups) Medjool dates, stoned
- 150g (about 1¼ cups) soft dried figs, stalks removed
- 100g (about ¾ cup) soft dried prunes, stoned
- 100g (about ⅔ cup) dried apricots
- 100g (about ¾ cup) currants, dried cranberries or sultanas
- zest and juice of 1 large orange
- 175g (¾ cup plus 1 tsp) butter
- 300g (1 cup) condensed milk
- 175ml (¾ cup) freshly brewed black tea
- 75g (½ cup plus 1 Tbsp) wholemeal (whole wheat) or rye flour
- ½ tsp baking powder
- ½ tsp bicarbonate of soda (baking soda)
- ½ tsp salt
- 2 Tbsp apricot jam (jelly) mixed with 2 Tbsp boiling water

Egg-free saffron and pistachio cake

Growing up, suji ka halwa (semolina pudding) was made for any occasion. No festivities were complete without it. I remember my mother making a big mound of it and placing a candle over it to make a birthday cake. Many Middle Eastern and European cultures have similar puddings, some with eggs, some drenched with lots of syrup. My version is an attempt at making those childhood puddings in cake form.

1 First, combine all the syrup ingredients in a pan and bring to a gentle simmer for 8–10 minutes, until it has a thin, honey-like texture. Set aside.

2 Oil and flour a 20cm (8in) round cake tin with sides 5cm (2in) deep. Line the base with a disc of baking paper. Preheat the oven to 170°C fan/190°C/375°F/Gas mark 5.

3 Put the saffron in a small bowl, slightly crush the strands and stir in the 2 Tbsp of milk.

4 Add the vegetable oil or butter and milk to a small jug. Stir and set aside.

5 Sift the semolina, flour, caster sugar, baking powder, bicarbonate of soda, salt, ground almonds, ground pistachios and ground cardamom into a large bowl. Using a balloon whisk, stir the dry mixture until well-combined.

6 Make a well in the centre of the dry ingredients. Pour in the milk and the butter or oil. Add the saffron milk and rose water. Using a balloon whisk, stir until just combined and you have a smooth batter. Do not overmix.

7 Pour the mixture into the prepared tin. Tap the tin gently on the worktop to release any air pockets. Bake for 45–50 minutes, or until the surface is springy to touch and a skewer comes out clean. It will be golden on top with a few cracks.

8 Cool the cake for 10 minutes in the tin, then turn out on a wire rack. Brush with the sugar syrup while the cake is still slightly warm. Allow to cool completely.

9 Meanwhile, mix all the glaze ingredients together until you have a vibrant yellow glaze with a thick pouring consistency.

10 Once the cake is completely cool, pour over the glaze. Sprinkle with edible petals and pistachio nibs, if you like.

- 75ml (½ cup) sunflower oil or 100g (⅓ cup) butter, melted then slightly cooled, plus extra for greasing
- 100g (½ cup plus 2 Tbsp) plain (all-purpose) flour, plus extra for dusting
- 10–15 saffron strands
- 325ml (1¼ cups plus 2 Tbsp) milk, plus 2 Tbsp
- 200g (2 cups) superfine semolina
- 180g (¾ cup plus 2 Tbsp) golden caster (superfine) sugar
- 1½ tsp baking powder
- ½ tsp bicarbonate of soda (baking soda)
- ½ tsp salt
- 100g (about 1 cup) ground almonds
- 100g (about 1 cup) ground pistachios
- ½ tsp ground cardamom
- ½ tsp rose water

For the sugar syrup

- 75ml (¼ cup plus 1 Tbsp) water
- 75g (¼ cup plus 2 Tbsp) caster (superfine) sugar
- ¼ tsp salt
- 2 cadamom pods, slightly crushed
- 6–8 saffron strands
- 1 Tbsp lemon juice

For the glaze

- 100g (¾ cup plus 1½ Tbsp) sifted icing (confectioners') sugar
- 4 Tbsp water
- 10–12 saffron strands, crushed to a powder

To decorate (optional)

- edible flowers
- pistachio nibs

Egg-free berries and fresh cream cake

My mother loves all the summer berries we enjoy in the UK. Whenever she visits, she goes through punnets of fruit every day, filling her quota for a few years. My husband will bring home different kinds of berries for her, just to see her smile. It makes my heart melt. One year, I made this simple cake for her birthday: most vegetarian Indians don't eat eggs but are not vegan, consuming both honey and dairy products. You can double the mixture and bake two sponges for a sandwich cake, as pictured.

1 Butter and flour a 20cm (8in) round cake tin. Line the base with a disc of baking paper. Preheat the oven to 160°C fan/180°C/350°F/Gas mark 4.

2 Sift the flour, baking powder, bicarbonate of soda, sugar and salt into a large bowl, then mix in the ground almonds.

3 In another large bowl, combine the buttermilk, oil, butter, vanilla and condensed milk.

4 Pour the wet ingredients into the dry ingredients and stir until well combined. Do not overmix.

5 Pour the batter into the prepared tin. Bake for 40–45 minutes, or until a skewer comes out clean, the cake is well-risen and is springy to touch. Avoid opening the oven door until at least three-quarters of the cooking time has passed. Don't worry if the cake deflates slightly after baking.

6 Cool the cake for 10 minutes in the tin, then turn out onto a wire rack. Leave to cool completely.

7 When ready to serve, whip the cream to soft peaks, then add the icing sugar, vanilla and salt. Stir to combine.

8 Spoon the cream onto the cool cake. Dollop the jam over and add the berries.

9 Using a small tea strainer or sieve, sift the icing sugar over the sponge in an even layer to create a white dusting. Sprinkle over some petals and small edible flowers.

For the cake (double this for a sandwich cake; see intro)

- 75g (⅓ cup) butter, melted, plus extra for greasing
- 175g (1½ cups) plain (all-purpose) flour, plus extra for dusting
- 1½ tsp baking powder
- ½ tsp bicarbonate of soda
- 175g (scant 1 cup) golden caster (superfine) sugar
- ½ tsp salt
- 70g (about ¾ cup) ground almonds
- 75ml (¼ cup plus 2 Tbsp) buttermilk
- 100ml (7 Tbsp) sunflower oil
- 1 tsp vanilla extract
- 75g (¼ cup) condensed milk

For the filling

- 250ml (1 cup) double (heavy) cream, whipped to soft peaks
- 3 Tbsp icing (confectioners') sugar
- 1 tsp vanilla extract
- ½ tsp salt
- 4 Tbsp strawberry or raspberry jam (jelly)
- handful of seasonal berries (raspberries, blackberries, strawberries)

To decorate

- 2 Tbsp icing (confectioners') sugar
- edible flowers (optional)

Vegan chocolate cake

When wedding cakes became a big part of my baking journey, requests for a vegan layer or a full vegan cake were becoming more common. My instinctive method of baking always starts with butter and eggs, so this was something that I needed to figure out fast – without compromising on the flavour, taste or texture of my much-loved, award-winning chocolate cake. My vegan option had to match the standard of that chocolate cake, and it is surprisingly good. You don't have to be vegan to enjoy this cake.

1 Oil and flour two 20cm (8in) round cake tins. Line the bases with discs of baking paper. Preheat the oven to 160°C fan/180°C/350°F/Gas mark 4.

Tip I recommend using 2 tins here for a better bake. If you only have one, pour half the batter into the tin, then bake and turn out the cake as per the recipe. Oil and flour the tin again, re-line the base, then pour in the remaining batter and bake.

2 This method does not use any sort of mixer, like my chocolate cake you just need a couple of large bowls and a large metal spoon or spatula.

3 Sift the flour, sugars, cocoa and salt into a large bowl.

4 In the second bowl, mix the oil, milk, vanilla and hot coffee. Give it all a stir.

5 Pour the wet ingredients over the dry ingredients. Fold together, using a large spoon or spatula, until just combined. Do not overmix the batter.

6 Mix the bicarbonate of soda and vinegar in a small cup or bowl. They will froth up. Immediately pour this into the prepared batter, and mix it in. Now quickly divide the batter, equally, between both tins.

7 Bake for 25–28 minutes, checking within 25 minutes, until a skewer comes out clean and the cake is springy to touch.

8 Leave the cakes to cool in the tins for about 10 minutes. Turn out both cakes onto a wire rack to cool completely.

Continued...

- 100ml (7 Tbsp) sunflower oil, plus extra for greasing
- 250g (1¾ cups plus 2 Tbsp) plain (all-purpose) flour, plus extra for dusting
- 150g (¾ cup plus 1 Tbsp) golden caster (superfine) sugar
- 100g (about ½ cup) soft brown sugar
- 50g (½ cup) cocoa powder
- ½ tsp salt
- 75ml (5 Tbsp) almond or oat milk
- 1 tsp vanilla extract
- 2 Tbsp instant coffee granules mixed with 200ml (¾ cup plus 1 Tbsp) boiling water
- 1½ tsp bicarbonate of soda (baking soda)
- 30ml (2 Tbsp) white vinegar
- 1 batch Chocolate Glaze (page 51)

For the chocolate buttercream

- 200g (¾ cup plus 2 Tbsp) dairy-free vegan butter
- 200g (1¾ cups) sifted icing (confectioners') sugar
- 1 tsp vanilla extract
- ½ salt
- 50g (½ cup) cocoa powder
- 150g (5½oz) dark chocolate (70% cocoa), melted and cooled

9 Meanwhile, make the chocolate glaze, following the method on page 51.

10 To make the buttercream, whisk the vegan butter using a paddle or beater attachment or a hand-held beater for 2–3 minutes, until it is lightly whipped and fluffy. Add the sifted icing sugar, 2–3 spoonfuls at a time, whisking it at medium to high speed, after each addition. Keep tasting it as you may not need all of the icing sugar. Once it is to your liking, add the vanilla, salt and cocoa. Whisk again for a minute or so. Finally, pour in the melted and cooled chocolate. Keep whisking on a slow speed until it is well combined and fluffy.

Assembly

11 Double-line a 20cm (8in) round cake tin with cling film (plastic wrap), allowing a slight overhang.

12 Slice each cake horizontally in half so that you have 4 discs.

13 Place the first disc in the lined cake tin. Add 2–3 tablespoons of the chocolate buttercream, spreading it evenly. Place a second cake disc in the tin and repeat with the buttercream. Repeat with the remaining cake discs and the buttercream, finishing with a layer of chocolate cake on top.

14 Cover the cake with an extra piece of cling film so that the top is covered and place the tin in the freezer for 1 hour.

15 When ready to serve, take the cake out of the freezer. Ease the cake out of the tin with the help of the cling film.

16 Discard all the cling film and set the cake on a 20cm (8in) cake stand over a wire rack.

17 If the chocolate glaze has cooled, warm it slightly over a medium heat. Pour the glaze over the cake.

18 Leave the cake at room temperature, to allow the glaze to harden.

19 Decorate the cake with edible flowers and chocolate curls, if you wish.

To decorate (optional)

- edible flowers
- chocolate curls

Gluten-free chocolate torte with blackberries

When the leaves are turning and winter is around the corner, baking this cake helps me to let go of summer and prepare for the colder seasons. I love to go on early autumn walks to pick blackberries for the topping, which makes this cake extra-special (though it is delicious as it is!).

With so few components, good-quality ingredients make all the difference to this cake. If you can't take the bitterness of dark chocolate, substitute half with milk chocolate.

1 Butter and dust a 20cm (8in) springform or loose-bottomed tin with cocoa powder. If you don't have one, line a standard 20cm (8in) tin with a large piece of baking paper, pressing it on all sides, and allowing an overhang. Preheat the oven to 170°C fan/190°C/375°F/Gas mark 5.

2 Place the butter and chocolate in a heatproof bowl over a pan of barely simmering water. Let it melt. Add the coffee and salt. Stir. Once incorporated, remove from the heat and leave to cool slightly.

3 Spread the almonds on a large baking tray and toast for 7–8 minutes. Keep an eye on them as they can burn easily.

4 Remove from the oven and, once cool, finely chop the almonds (or use a food processor for this if you have one).

5 Put the egg whites into a large bowl if using a hand-held whisk, or a stand mixer with the whisk attachment. Whisk until soft peaks form. With the whisk still running, gradually add half the sugar, spoon by spoon, until you have a thick and glossy meringue. Set aside.

6 In a separate bowl, beat the egg yolks and add in the remaining sugar, until the mixture becomes pale and thick. Gently pour in the chocolate and butter mixture and give it a stir. Add the chopped almonds and vanilla. Gently stir using a spatula.

Continued...

- 200g (¾ cup plus 2 Tbsp) butter, diced, plus extra for greasing
- cocoa powder, for dusting
- 150g (5½oz) dark chocolate (55% cocoa), roughly chopped
- 2 Tbsp instant or ground coffee mixed with 2 Tbsp water
- ¼ tsp salt
- 200g (about 2 cups) whole unskinned almonds
- 4 eggs, separated
- 200g (1 cup) golden caster (superfine) sugar
- 1 tsp vanilla extract

For the topping (optional)

- 150g (about 1½ cups) blackberries
- 4 Tbsp golden caster sugar
- 15g (2 Tbsp) sifted icing (confectioners') sugar
- 150ml (½ cup plus 1 Tbsp) double (heavy) cream
- ½ tsp vanilla bean paste
- chocolate shavings
- cocoa powder, for dusting
- edible flowers

7 Now add 2 large spoonfuls of the meringue to the egg and almond mixture. Mix well until the mixture has lightened a little. Add the rest of the meringue in 2–3 goes, gently folding in after each addition. Be careful not to deflate the batter.

8 Pour the batter into the prepared tin. Tap the tin gently on the worktop to release any air pockets. Bake for 35–40 minutes. The top sometimes cracks a little but that's okay. Test the cake with a skewer: it should come out clean with a few crumbs clinging to it but no liquid. Chocolate cakes are better slightly underbaked.

9 Cool the cake for 10 minutes in the tin, then lift it out onto a wire rack. Remove the baking paper.

10 The cake is ready to enjoy as it is, dusted with some cocoa powder. Alternatively, to make the topping, sprinkle the blackberries with the caster sugar. Give them a gentle stir and leave aside for 10–15 minutes. Meanwhile, whip the icing sugar, cream and vanilla until soft peaks form. Spoon it over the cooled cake, then top with the macerated blackberries, any leftover juices and some chocolate shavings. A light dusting of cocoa and a few edible flowers add to its beauty.

Gluten-free plum and blueberry cake

When I started selling at markets, I wanted to make something a gluten-free option that would appeal to everyone. My first ever market was in September and autumn was setting in. Plums were in season. I sold it as an almond, plum and blueberry cake – not as a 'free-from' cake – but if anyone asked for gluten-free, they had this option. It went down so well. If you do not need this to be gluten-free, you can make it with self-raising wheat flour.

1 Butter and flour a 20cm (8in) round cake tin. Line the base and sides with baking paper, allowing an overhang. (Or use a springform or loose-bottomed tin and line the base with a disc of baking paper.) Preheat the oven to 170°C fan/190°C/375°F/ Gas mark 5.

2 Sift the flour and salt into a large bowl and mix in the ground almonds.

3 Break the eggs into a small jug and gently mix using a fork.

4 Put the butter and the 2 sugars in a large bowl and whisk until pale and fluffy. Add the eggs in 3 goes, beating well after each addition. Now add the dry ingredients in 3–4 goes and gently fold in using a spatula, followed by the vanilla, soured cream and half the blueberries. Give the batter a final stir.

5 Pour the batter into the prepared tin and level with the back of a spoon. Arrange the plums, cut sides up, on top of the batter, pressing them in gently. Scatter the remaining blueberries over the top, then sprinkle with demerara sugar. Tap the tin gently on the worktop to release any air pockets.

6 Bake for 40–45 minutes, or until a skewer comes out clean. After 30 minutes, cover with a piece of foil if the top is browning too much.

7 Leave the cake in the tin for 10 minutes, then gently lift it out with the help of the paper overhang. Place it on a wire rack. Remove the paper and let it cool completely.

8 Dust the sides with sifted icing sugar and top with fresh blueberries and a few edible flowers, if you wish. It makes a great snacking cake with tea or coffee, or served warm with lots of custard it becomes dessert for autumn evenings.

- 150g (⅔ cup) butter, plus extra for greasing
- 125g (1 cup minus 1 Tbsp) gluten-free self-raising flour, plus extra for dusting
- ½ tsp salt
- 180g (1¾ cups plus 3 Tbsp) ground almonds
- 5 eggs
- 150g (¾ cup plus 1 Tbsp) golden caster (superfine) sugar
- 75g (6 Tbsp) soft brown sugar
- 1 tsp vanilla bean paste
- 50ml (3 Tbsp) soured cream
- 150g (about 1½ cups) blueberries
- 6 small ripe plums, halved and stoned
- 50g (¼ cup) demerara (raw brown) sugar, for sprinkling

To decorate
- 2 Tbsp sifted icing (confectioners') sugar
- blueberries
- edible flowers (optional)

Vegan lemon and pistachio cake

Lemon and pistachio are two of my favourite ingredients. When one of my friends went vegan, she said one of the things she missed most was my lemon cake. That's when I started to work on this cake. This recipe results in a thinner cake but it does not compromise on flavour. Look for a mild, good-quality extra virgin olive oil – it makes all the difference!

1 Oil and flour a 20cm (8in) round cake tin with sides 5cm (2in) deep. Line the base with a disc of baking paper. Preheat the oven to 160°C fan/180°C/350°F/Gas mark 4.

2 Sift the flour, cornflour, baking powder, bicarbonate of soda, sugar and salt into a large bowl. Stir through the chopped pistachios.

3 Put the milk, olive oil, lemon zest and juice, and vanilla into a medium jug. Stir together.

4 Pour the wet ingredients into the dry ingredients. Stir with a wooden spoon or spatula until the batter just comes together. Do not overmix.

5 Pour the batter into the prepared tin. Tap the tin gently on the worktop to release any air pockets. Bake for 40–45 minutes, or until a skewer comes out clean, the cake is well-risen and springy to touch

6 Allow the cake cool in the tin for about 10 minutes. Turn out onto a wire rack to cool completely.

7 Meanwhile, make the glaze. Mix the sifted icing sugar, lemon zest and juice and salt together to make a thick glaze. Pour over the cooled cake and sprinkle edible flowers and pistachios (if using).

- 125ml (½ cup) extra virgin olive oil, plus extra for greasing
- 200g (1½ cups) plain (all-purpose) flour, plus extra for dusting
- 25g (¼ cup) cornflour (cornstarch)
- 1 tsp baking powder
- ½ tsp bicarbonate of soda (baking soda)
- 150g (¾ cup plus 1 Tbsp) golden caster (superfine) sugar
- ¼ tsp salt
- 100g (about 1 cup) pistachios, finely chopped in a spice grinder
- 150ml (½ cup plus 1 Tbsp) vegan milk
- zest and juice of 3 lemons
- 1 tsp vanilla extract

For the glaze

- 150g (1¼ cups) sifted icing (confectioners') sugar
- zest and juice of 1 lemon
- pinch of salt

To decorate (optional)

- edible flowers
- pistachio nuts to sprinkle

Gluten-free pistachio and raspberry friand cake

Friands are the first small bakes I started making to order and for large events and dessert tables. I have lost the count of the number of times and batches I have baked of this cake. It is my go-to recipe to take as a gift.

1 Butter and flour a 20cm (8in) round cake tin. Line the base and sides with baking paper, allowing an overhang. Preheat the oven to 170°C fan/190°C/375°F/Gas mark 5.

2 Toss the raspberries in the 2 tablespoons of flour. Set aside.

3 Put the egg whites in a medium, very clean bowl. Whisk until foamy using a balloon whisk. We just need to loosen the egg whites so do not overwhisk; some foam and liquid in the base of the bowl is okay. Set aside.

4 Sift the flour, icing sugar and salt into a large bowl and mix in the almonds.

5 Pour the warm melted brown butter into the dry ingredients. Add the vanilla and lemon zest. Give it a good stir: this will be a dry crumbly mix.

6 Fold in the egg whites in 3 goes, stirring with a large metal spoon after each addition until just combined. Do not overmix.

7 Pour half the batter into the prepared tin. Dot in half the flour-coated raspberries. Pour in the rest of the batter. Top with the remaining raspberries and sprinkle the flaked almond flakes in an even layer. Sift over the extra icing sugar. Tap the tin gently on the worktop to release any air pockets.

8 Bake for 30 minutes, or until a skewer comes out clean.

9 Leave the cake in the tin for 10 minutes, then gently lift it with the help of the overhang and place on a wire rack to cool.

10 For the raspberry glaze, follow the method on page 50, sifting in the raspberry powder with the sugar. Once the cake is cooled completely, drizzle the cake with the glaze and finish with extra fresh raspberries and edible flowers, if you wish.

11 This cake can be served any time, for breakfast, with tea or for picnics. It can also be served warm as dessert with a large dollop of clotted cream or custard and extra raspberries.

- butter, for greasing
- 75g (½ cup plus 1 Tbsp) gluten-free self-raising (self-rising) flour, plus 2 Tbsp, plus extra for dusting
- 150g (about 1½ cups) raspberries, plus extra to decorate
- 140g (⅔ cup minus 2 tsp) Brown Butter (page 46), from 175g (¾ cup plus 1 tsp) butter, still warm
- 175g (6oz) egg whites (5 large eggs)
- 200g (1¾ cups) sifted icing (confectioners') sugar, plus 2 Tbsp
- ¼ tsp salt
- 150g (1½ cups) ground almonds
- 1 tsp vanilla bean paste
- zest of 2 lemons
- 75g (about 1 cup) flaked (slivered) almonds
- edible flowers (optional)

For the raspberry glaze

- 1 batch of Icing Sugar Drizzle (page 50)
- pinch of salt
- 20g (1 Tbsp plus 1 tsp) freeze-dried raspberry powder

<u>Variations</u>

The batter will also make 12 individual friands. Divide the batter in a 12-hole friand or deep cupcake tin and reduce the baking time to 20–22 minutes.

This also works well with blackberries.

Buttercream cakes

Buttercream cakes became the workhorse of sorts of my little baking business. For four years before I began my business, I was practising these cakes at almost every birthday and celebration for friends and family, as a hobby baker.

I had come across American baking books with photos of buttercream cakes and started to work on a few recipes, finding buttercream to be a good and stable medium for decorating. But the result was overly sweet, and I didn't fancy eating whipped vegetable fat, which is what most recipes called for. Over the years, I managed to make buttercream less sweet and gritty, using natural ingredients and good-quality butter. But I still was not convinced.

Then I came across French-, German- and Swiss-style buttercreams. I had many failed attempts, but there was something about Swiss meringue

buttercream that made me keep trying. Once I got it right, I knew I had found my medium: it's light, not too sweet, stable enough to use as a filling or for finishing celebration cakes – even wedding cakes – and it takes flavours well. It is a little tricky to master but you will find the steps and all my tips on pages 52–3. You will be amazed how good it is.

In this chapter, I have shared eight of my favourite flavour options, but you can mix and match to create your own bespoke combinations.

Note: You **must** allow time for buttercream cakes to chill completely, for a minimum of 2 hours, up to 24 hours. Once assembled, cut the cake chilled, but serve at room temperature.

All of these cakes will store for up to 3 days in the fridge.

Rose, raspberry and pistachio cake

*This is a popular flavour combination for a
wedding. I catered for a
wedding for a London chef, who mentioned that this cake was one
of the best things he had eaten that year. It happens to be one of my
favourites too. If you just want a snacking cake, you can just make
the sponge and finish it with a rose water glaze.*

1 Butter and flour a 20cm (8in) round cake tin. Line the
base with a disc of baking paper. Preheat the oven to
160°C fan/180°C/350°F/Gas mark 4.

2 Sift the flour, baking powder and salt into a bowl. Stir in
the ground pistachios.

3 Break the eggs into a small jug and stir with a fork.

4 Put the butter, sugar and pistachio paste in a large bowl
if using a hand-held beater, or a stand mixer with a beater
attachment, and cream for about 6–8 minutes, or until the
mixture is pale and fluffy.

5 Add the eggs in 3–4 goes, beating well after each addition.
Add the vanilla, rose water and soured cream, and mix well.
Add the dry ingredients in 3–4 goes, folding in gently after
each addition.

6 Pour the batter into the prepared tin. Tap the tin
gently on the worktop to release any air pockets. Bake
for 35–40 minutes, or until the surface is springy to touch
and a skewer comes out clean.

7 Cool the cake for 10 minutes in the tin, then turn out onto
a wire rack.

8 Once cooled, slice into 3 horizontal cake discs.

9 To make the buttercream, whip the Swiss meringue
buttercream with the pistachio paste until it is a beautiful
green colour. Divide into 2 bowls: one for filling, one
for coating.

Continued...

- 250g (1 cup plus 2 Tbsp) butter,
  plus extra for greasing
- 250g (1¾ cups plus 2 Tbsp) plain
  (all-purpose) flour, plus extra for dusting
- 1½ tsp baking powder
- ¼ tsp salt
- 125g (about 1 cup) pistachios,
  powdered in a spice grinder
- 5 eggs
- 250g (1⅓ cups plus 1 Tbsp) golden caster
  (superfine) sugar
- 50g pistachio paste (optional)
- 1 tsp vanilla bean paste
- 1 tsp rose water
- 75ml (5 Tbsp) soured cream

**For the pistachio Swiss meringue
buttercream**

- 1 batch of Swiss Meringue Buttercream
  (pages 52–3)
- 75g (5 Tbsp) pistachio paste

For the filling

- 300g (scant 1 cup) seedless raspberry jam
  (jelly)
- 150g (about 1 cup) fresh raspberries

To decorate (optional)

- chopped pistachios
- edible flowers

Assembly

10 Wash and dry a 20cm (8in) round cake tin or use a springform cake tin. Line it with 2 layers of cling film (plastic wrap), allowing a 2cm (¾in) overhang.

11 Place one of the cake discs in the base of the tin. Add 5 tablespoons of pistachio buttercream and level using the back of a spoon. Add 2–3 tablespoons of raspberry jam, spreading it over the buttercream but leaving a 2.5cm (1in) gap around the rim of the tin. Scatter over a few fresh raspberries.

12 Place the second cake disc in the tin and repeat the layers of buttercream and jam as before.

13 Top with the third cake disc. Thinly spread a few tablespoons of the buttercream over the surface. Pull in the cling film over it.

14 Completely chill the cake for a minimum of 2 hours, or up to 24 hours in advance.

15 Once the cake has completely chilled, remove from the fridge, ease it out of the tin and take off the cling film. Place it on a suitable cake plate or cake board, then follow the instructions on page 34 for coating the cake using a cake turntable and a bench scraper.

16 Decorate the cake with a dusting of chopped pistachios and fresh or dried rose petals. Pipe on a few buttercream rosettes, if you like. Place it in the fridge to chill further for a few hours.

Coconut, lime and pineapple cake

Coconut, lime and pineapple has to be one of the best flavour combinations. This also happens to be a popular choice for summer weddings. I love these flavours so I enjoy making these cakes.

1 Butter and flour 20cm (8in) round cake tin. Line the base with a disc of baking paper. Preheat the oven to 170°C fan/190°C/375°F/Gas mark 5.

2 Sift the flour, baking powder and salt into a large bowl. Mix in the desiccated coconut.

3 Break the eggs into a small jug and gently stir with a fork.

4 Put the butter, coconut cream and sugar in a large bowl if using a wooden spoon or hand-held beater, or a stand mixer with a beater attachment. Cream for 6–8 minutes, or until the mixture is pale and fluffy.

5 Add the eggs in 3–4 goes, beating after each addition. Add in the vanilla extract, lime zest and juice, and soured cream. Mix well. Sift in the dry ingredients in 3–4 goes, folding in after each addition.

6 Pour the batter into the prepared tin. Tap the tin gently on the worktop to release any air pockets. Bake for 35–40 minutes, or until the surface is springy to touch and a skewer comes out clean.

7 Cool the cake for 10 minutes in the tin, then turn out onto a wire rack.

8 Once cooled, slice horizontally into 3 discs.

9 While the cake is cooking, make the pineapple compôte. Put the chopped pineapple, lime zest and juice, sugar and salt in a pan over a medium heat. Cook for 8–10 minutes, or until the pineapple has softened. Stir in the cornflour paste and cook for a further 2–3 minutes. Remove from the heat and let it cool completely.

10 To make the coconut buttercream, whip the Swiss meringue buttercream with the lime zest and coconut cream. Divide into 2 bowls: one for filling, one for coating.

Continued...

- 200g (¾ cup plus 2 Tbsp) butter, plus extra for greasing
- 250g (1¾ cups plus 2 Tbsp) plain (all-purpose) flour, plus extra for dusting
- 1 tsp baking powder
- ¼ tsp salt
- 75g (about 1 cup) desiccated (shredded) coconut
- 4 eggs
- 50g (1¾oz) coconut cream (not milk)
- 200g (generous 1 cup) caster (superfine) sugar
- 1 tsp vanilla extract
- zest and juice of 1 lime
- 75ml (5 Tbsp) soured cream

For the pineapple compôte
- 1 medium pineapple, peeled, cored and finely chopped
- zest and juice of 1 lime
- 50g (¼ cup) caster (superfine) sugar
- 1 tsp salt
- 1 tsp cornflour (cornstarch) mixed with 1 Tbsp water

For the coconut buttercream
- 1 batch of Swiss Meringue Buttercream (pages 52–3)
- zest of 2 limes
- 50g (1¾oz) coconut cream (not milk)

To decorate
- edible flowers (optional)
- dehydrated pineapple flowers (see tip)
- coconut flakes

Assembly

11 Wash and dry a 20cm (8in) round cake tin or use a springform cake tin. Line it with 2 layers of cling film (plastic wrap), allowing a 2cm (¾in) overhang.

12 Place one of the cake discs in the base of the tin. Add 5 tablespoons of the coconut buttercream and level using the back of a spoon. Add 2–3 tablespoons of pineapple compôte, spreading it slightly over the buttercream but leaving a 2.5cm (1 in) gap around the rim of the tin.

13 Place the second cake disc in the tin and repeat the layers of buttercream and compôte, as above.

14 Top with the third cake disc. Thinly spread a few tablespoons of the buttercream over the surface. Pull in the cling film over it.

15 Completely chill the cake for a minimum of 2 hours, or up to 24 hours in advance.

16 Once the cake has completely chilled, remove from the fridge, ease it out of the tin and take off the cling film. Place it on a suitable cake plate or cake board, then follow the instructions on page 34 for coating the cake using a cake turntable and a bench scraper.

17 Decorate the cake with fresh or dried edible flowers, dehydrated pineapple flowers and coconut flakes. Place it in the fridge to chill further for a few hours.

Tip To make dehydrated pineapple 'flowers', you can dry thinly sliced pineapple rings an oven at 90°C fan/ 110°C/225°F/Gas mark ¼ for 3 –4 hours. You can also buy dehydrated pineapple rings, used in the cocktail industry.

Tahini and autumn berries cake

As a concept in my head, tahini and autumn berries worked really well because sesame, the main ingredient of tahini, has warming qualities that suit the cooler days. Autumn also brings blackberries, which I find pair beautifully with the tahini. I have added some blueberry jam to give extra depth and sweetness.

---

1 Butter and flour a 20cm (8in) round cake tin. Line the base with a disc of baking paper. Preheat the oven to 170°C fan/190°C/375°F/Gas mark 5.

2 Sift the flour, baking powder and salt into a bowl.

3 Break the eggs into a small jug and stir with a fork.

4 Put the butter, sugar and tahini in a large bowl if using a hand-held beater, or a stand mixer with a beater attachment. Cream for about 6–8 minutes, or until the mixture is pale and fluffy.

5 Add the eggs in 3–4 goes, beating well after each addition. Add the vanilla and mix well. Add the flour mixture in 3–4 goes. Stir in the soured cream.

6 Pour the batter into the prepared tin. Tap the tin gently on the worktop to release any air pockets. Bake for 35–40 minutes, or until the surface is springy to touch and a skewer comes out clean.

7 Meanwhile, make the buttercream. Whisk the Swiss meringue buttercream with the blackberry powder, tahini and a pinch of salt. Divide into 2 bowls: one for filling, one for coating.

8 For the filling, mix together the 2 jams and halve any blackberries that are large.

9 Cool the cake for 10 minutes in the tin, then turn out onto a wire rack.

10 Once cooled, slice into 3 horizontal cake discs.

Continued...

- 200g (¾ cup plus 2 Tbsp) butter, plus extra for greasing
- 250g (1¾ cups plus 2 Tbsp) plain (all-purpose) flour, plus extra for dusting
- 1 tsp baking powder
- ¼ tsp salt
- 4 eggs
- 200g (generous 1 cup) caster (superfine) sugar
- 75g (about ⅓ cup) tahini
- 1 tsp vanilla bean paste
- 75ml (5 Tbsp) soured cream

For the blackberry buttercream

- 1 batch of Swiss Meringue Buttercream (pages 52–3)
- 30g (2 Tbsp) sifted freeze-dried blackberry powder
- 50g (about ¼ cup) tahini
- ½ tsp salt

For the filling

- 100g (about ⅓ cup) blueberry conserve
- 100g (about ⅓ cup) blackberry conserve
- 150g (generous 1 cup) fresh blackberries

To decorate (optional)

- edible flowers
- sesame seeds

Assembly

11 Wash and dry a 20cm (8in) round cake tin or use a springform cake tin. Line it with 2 layers of cling film (plastic wrap), allowing a 2cm (¾in) overhang.

12 Place one of the cake discs in the base of the tin. Add 5 tablespoons of the blackberry buttercream and level using the back of a spoon. Add 2–3 tablespoons of the jam filling, spreading it over the buttercream but leaving a 2.5cm (1 in) gap around the rim of the tin. Scatter over a few fresh blackberries.

13 Place the second cake layer in the tin and repeat the layers of buttercream, jam filling and blackberries, as above.

14 Place the third cake disc on top. Thinly spread a few tablespoons of the buttercream over the surface. Pull in the cling film over it.

15 Completely chill the cake for a minimum of 2 hours, or up to 24 hours in advance.

16 Once the cake has completely chilled, remove from the fridge, ease it out of the tin and take off the cling film. Place it on a suitable cake plate or cake board, then follow the instructions on page 34 for coating the cake using a cake turntable and a bench scraper.

17 Decorate the cake with edible flowers and a sprinkling of sesame seeds. Place it in the fridge to chill further for a few hours.

Chai masala and pear cake

Pear is a very neutral-tasting fruit, which means it absorbs the flavour of spices well. I especially like to make this cake in winter. Over the years, I have baked this as an alternative Christmas cake to order.

Every Indian home has their own chai masala blend. This one is borrowed from my parent's kitchen and, over the years, it has become mine. This recipe makes enough for the cake below, but you can double it and store it to sprinkle over your granola or porridge, or to make masala chai.

---

1 To make the chai masala, simply grind everything together (easiest in a spice grinder).

2 Butter and flour a 20cm (8in) round cake tin. Line the base with a disc of baking paper. Preheat the oven to 160°C fan/180°C/350°F/Gas mark 4.

3 Sift the flour, baking powder, chai masala, sugar and salt into a large bowl if using a hand-held beater, or a stand mixer with a beater attachment. Give it a quick mix.

4 Add in the butter and beat until it forms a sandy breadcrumb-like texture.

5 Put the soured cream, eggs and vanilla in a small jug and whisk using a fork. Pour this liquid into the bowl in 3–4 goes, mixing after each addition.

6 Pour the batter into the prepared tin. Tap the tin gently on the worktop to release any air pockets. Bake for 45–55 minutes, or until a skewer comes out clean and the cake starts to shrink from the edges of the tin.

7 Cool the cake for 10 minutes in the tin, then turn out onto a wire rack.

8 Once cooled, slice horizontally into 3 discs.

9 Meanwhile, make the pear compôte. Put the chopped pears, sugar, spices, butter and salt in a small pan over a gentle heat. Cook for about 10–15 minutes until the pears are soft and mushy, but still holding their shape. Stir in the cornflour paste and cook for a further 2–3 minutes. It should be a thick jam-like consistency. Turn off the heat.

Continued...

- 250g (¾ cup plus 2 Tbsp) butter, plus extra for greasing
- 250g (1¾ cups plus 2 Tbsp) plain (all-purpose) flour, plus extra for dusting
- 1½ tsp baking powder
- 1 Tbsp chai masala powder (see below)
- 250g (generous 1 cup) golden caster (superfine) sugar
- ½ tsp salt
- 100ml (7 Tbsp) soured cream
- 5 eggs
- 1 tsp vanilla extract

For the chai masala
- 10 whole green cardamom pods
- 2 whole black cardamom pods
- 10 black peppercorns
- 6 cloves
- 8cm (3in) stick of cinnamon
- 1 Tbsp ground ginger
- ½ Tbsp freshly grated nutmeg
- 1 Tbsp black tea leaves

10 To make the chai masala buttercream, whisk the Swiss meringue buttercream, chai masala and salted caramel until well combined. Divide into 2 bowls: one for filling, one for coating.

Assembly

11 Wash and dry a 20cm (8in) round cake tin or use a springform cake tin. Line it with 2 layers of cling film (plastic wrap), allowing a 2cm (¾in) overhang.

12 Place one of the cake discs in the base of the tin. Add 5 tablespoons of the chai masala buttercream and level using the back of a spoon. Add 2–3 tablespoons of pear compôte, spreading it over the buttercream but leaving a 2cm (¾in) gap around the rim of the cake tin. Drizzle in 2 tablespoons of salted caramel.

13 Place the second cake disc in the tin and repeat the layers of buttercream, compôte and caramel drizzle as above.

14 Top with the third cake disc. Thinly spread a few tablespoons of the buttercream over the the surface. Pull in the cling film over it.

15 Completely chill the cake for a minimum of 2 hours, or up to 24 hours in advance.

16 Once the cake has completely chilled, remove from the fridge, ease it out of the tin and take off the cling film. Place it on a suitable cake plate or cake board, then follow the instructions on page 34 for coating the cake using a cake turntable and a bench scraper.

17 Decorate the cake with fresh or dried edible flowers. Place it in the fridge to chill further for a few hours.

For the pear compôte

- 5 pears, peeled, cored and finely chopped
- 100g (generous ½ cup) golden caster (superfine) sugar
- 1 Tbsp chai masala (see above)
- ¼ tsp freshly grated nutmeg
- 50g (3½ Tbsp) butter
- 1 tsp salt
- 1 tsp cornflour (cornstarch) mixed with 1 Tbsp water

For the chai masala buttercream

- 1 batch of Swiss Meringue Buttercream (pages 52–3)
- 1 Tbsp chai masala
- 50g (1¾oz) salted caramel

For the filling

- 100g (3½oz) salted caramel

To decorate (optional)

- edible flowers

Blueberry, pistachio and lemon cake

This is one of the first buttercream cakes I made. I have been making it on repeat ever since. Blueberry purée gives a beautiful lilac colour to the buttercream while pistachios impart their green colour to the sponge. Together the combination looks beautiful.

1 Butter and flour a 20cm (8in) round cake tin. Line the base with a disc of baking paper. Preheat the oven to 160°C fan/180°C/350°F/Gas mark 4.

2 Sift the flour, baking powder, salt and powdered pistachios into a large bowl.

3 Break the eggs into a small jug and stir until just mixed.

4 Put the butter, pistachio paste and sugar in a large bowl if using a hand-held beater, or a stand mixer with a beater attachment. Beat for about 6–8 minutes, or until the mixture is pale and fluffy. Now add the eggs in 3–4 goes, incorporating well after each addition. Fold in the vanilla, lemon zest and juice and soured cream. Add the sifted dry ingredients in 3–4 goes, gently folding in after each addition.

5 Pour the batter into the prepared cake tin. Tap the tin gently on the worktop to release any air pockets. Bake for 35–40 minutes, or until the surface is springy to touch and a skewer comes out clean.

6 Cool the cake for 10 minutes in the tin, then turn out onto a wire rack.

7 Once cooled, slice horizontally into 4 discs.

8 To make the buttercream, whip the Swiss meringue buttercream with the blueberry conserve until it is a beautiful lilac colour. Divide into 2 bowls: one for filling, one for coating.

Continued...

- 250g (1 cup plus 2 Tbsp) butter, plus extra for greasing
- 250g (1¾ cups plus 2 Tbsp) plain (all-purpose) flour, plus extra for dusting
- 1½ tsp baking powder
- ¼ tsp salt
- 125g (about 1 cup) pistachios, powdered in a spice grinder
- 5 eggs
- 50g (5 Tbsp) pistachio paste (optional)
- 250g (1⅓ cups plus 1 Tbsp) golden caster (superfine) sugar
- 1 Tbsp vanilla bean paste
- zest and juice of 2 lemons
- 75ml (5 Tbsp) soured cream

For the blueberry Swiss meringue buttercream

- 1 batch of Swiss Meringue Buttercream (pages 52–3)
- 50g (about 3 Tbsp) blueberry conserve or compôte, puréed and sieved (strained)

For the filling

- 300g (scant 1 cup) blueberry conserve or compôte
- 150g (generous 1 cup) fresh blueberries

Assembly

9 Wash and dry a 20cm (8in) round cake tin or use a springform cake tin. Line it with 2 layers of cling film (plastic wrap), allowing a 2cm (¾in) overhang.

10 Place one of the cake discs in the base of the tin. Add 5 tablespoons of the blueberry buttercream and level using the back of a spoon. Add 2–3 tablespoons of the blueberry conserve, spreading it over the buttercream but leaving a 2.5cm (1in) gap around the rim of the tin. Scatter over a few fresh blueberries.

11 Place the second cake disc in the tin and repeat the layers of buttercream, conserve and fresh blueberries as before.

12 Top with the third cake disc. Thinly spread a few tablespoons of the buttercream over the surface. Pull in the cling film over it.

13 Completely chill the cake for a minimum of 2 hours, or up to 24 hours in advance.

14 Once the cake has completely chilled, remove from the fridge, ease it out of the tin and take off the cling film. Place it on a suitable cake plate or cake board, then follow the instructions on page 34 for coating the cake using a cake turntable and a bench scraper.

15 Decorate the cake with fresh or dried edible flowers and a dusting of chopped pistachios. Swirl with extra blueberry conserve, if you like. Place in the fridge to chill for a few more hours.

To decorate

· edible flowers (optional)
· chopped pistachios
· extra blueberry conserve

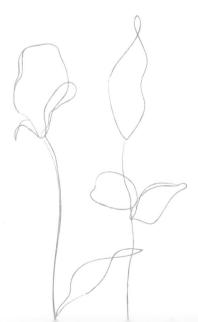

Lemon and elderflower cake

Long before it became a Royal Wedding cake, this was one of my most requested summer cakes. I make sure I make it for my family every summer too. It has all the freshness of lemon, and fragrance and subtle flavour from the elderflower.

1 Butter and flour a 20cm (8in) round cake tin and line the base with a disc of baking paper. Preheat the oven to 160°C fan/180°C/350°F/Gas mark 4.

2 Sift the flour, baking powder, icing sugar and salt into a large bowl.

3 Put the butter in a small pan over a low heat and melt until just liquid. Remove from the heat and let it cool slightly. Stir in the sunflower oil, lemon zest and juice, elderflower cordial, soured cream and vanilla. Add the eggs to this mixture and mix it well with a fork.

4 Pour the wet ingredients into the dry ingredients and mix to a smooth batter using a large wooden spoon or spatula.

5 Pour the batter into the prepared tin. Tap the tin gently on the worktop to release any air pockets. Bake for about 35–40 minutes, or until the surface is springy to touch and a skewer comes out clean.

6 Cool the cake for 10 minutes in the tin, then turn out onto a wire rack.

7 Once cooled, slice horizontally into 3 discs.

8 To make the buttercream, whisk the Swiss meringue buttercream with the lemon curd and the reduced elderflower and lemon cordial, until it is well combined. Divide into 2 bowls: one for filling, one for coating.

Continued...

- 200g (¾ cup plus 2 Tbsp) butter, plus extra for greasing
- 300g (2¼ cups) plain (all-purpose) flour, plus extra for dusting
- 1½ tsp baking powder
- 300g (2½ cups) sifted icing (confectioners') sugar
- ½ tsp salt
- 75ml (5 Tbsp) sunflower oil
- zest of 3 lemons and juice of 1 lemon
- 75ml (5 Tbsp) elderflower cordial (simmer over a gentle heat to reduce to 50ml/3 Tbsp plus 2 tsp)
- 100ml (7 Tbsp) soured cream
- 1 Tbsp vanilla bean paste
- 4 eggs

For the lemon and elderflower buttercream
- 1 batch of Swiss Meringue Buttercream (pages 52–3)
- 100g (3½oz) Lemon Curd (page 48)
- 75ml (5 Tbsp) elderflower cordial plus juice of 2 lemons (simmer over a gentle heat to reduce to 50ml/3 Tbsp plus 1 tsp)

For the filling
- 200g (7oz) Lemon Curd (page 48)

To decorate (optional)
- edible flowers

Assembly

9 Wash and dry a 20cm (8in) round cake tin or use a springform cake tin. Line it with 2 layers of cling film (plastic wrap), allowing a 2cm (¾in) overhang.

10 Place one of the cake discs in the base of the tin. Add 5 tablespoons of the lemon and elderflower buttercream and level using the back of a spoon. Add 2–3 tablespoons of lemon curd, spreading it over the buttercream but leaving a 2.5cm (1in) gap around the rim of the tin.

11 Place the second cake disc in the tin and repeat the layers of buttercream and curd as before.

12 Top with the third cake disc. Thinly spread a few tablespoons of the buttercream over the surface. Pull in the cling film over it.

13 Completely chill the cake for a minimum of 2 hours, or up to 24 hours in advance.

14 Once the cake has completely chilled, remove from the fridge, ease it out of the tin and take off the cling film. Place it on a suitable cake plate or cake board, then follow the instructions on page 34 for coating the cake using a cake turntable and a bench scraper.

15 Decorate the cake with fresh or dried edible flowers. Place in the fridge to chill for a few more hours.

Chocolate fudge buttercream cake

My chocolate fudge cake has its own following. Many families have been repeatedly ordering this cake for years. Baker friends have also complimented this cake and it has received a 'Great Taste' Award with 2 stars. Now that you have this recipe, you can make this cake on repeat too.

1 First make the ganache following the method on page 51. Set aside half for the cake filling.

2 Butter and dust with cocoa powder a 20cm (8in) round cake tin. Line the base with a disc of baking paper. Preheat the oven to 170°C fan/190°C/375°F/Gas mark 5.

3 Make the cake following steps 2–6 on page 72.

4 Bake for 35–40 minutes, or until a skewer comes out with a few crumbs clinging to it but not liquid; I find chocolate cakes are better slightly underbaked than overbaked.

5 Cool the cake for 10 minutes in the tin, then turn out onto a wire rack.

6 Meanwhile, whip the Swiss meringue buttercream with the remaining chocolate ganache and the cocoa until it is well combined. Divide into 2 bowls: one for filling, one for coating.

7 Once the cake is cooled, slice horizontally into 3 discs.

Assembly

8 Wash and dry a 20cm (8in) round cake tin or use a springform cake tin. Line it with 2 layers of cling film (plastic wrap), allowing a 2cm (¾in) overhang.

9 Place one of the cake discs in the base of the tin. Add 5 tablespoons of the chocolate buttercream and level using the back of a spoon. Add 2–3 tablespoons of the chocolate ganache, spreading it over the buttercream but leaving a 2.5cm (1in) gap around the rim of the tin.

Continued...

- 250g (1 cup plus 2 Tbsp) butter, plus extra for greasing
- 50g (½ cup) cocoa powder, plus extra for dusting
- 150g (5½oz) dark chocolate (70% cocoa), broken into pieces
- 150g (5½oz) milk chocolate, broken into pieces
- 150g (1 cup plus 2 Tbsp) plain (all-purpose) flour
- 1 tsp baking powder
- ½ tsp baking powder (baking soda)
- ¼ tsp salt
- 150g (¾ cup plus 1 Tbsp) golden caster (superfine) sugar
- 200g (1 cup) light soft brown sugar
- 4 large eggs
- 90ml (6 Tbsp) buttermilk
- 1 tsp vanilla extract
- 1 Tbsp instant coffee or medium-strength coffee dissolved in 125ml (½ cup) boiling water
- 1 batch of Chocolate Ganache (page 51)

For the chocolate Swiss meringue buttercream

- 1 batch of Swiss Meringue Buttercream (pages 52–3)
- ½ batch Chocolate Ganache (see above)
- 40g (scant ½ cup) cocoa powder

To decorate (optional)

- edible flowers

10 Place the second cake disc in the tin and repeat the layers of buttercream and ganache as before.

11 Top with the third disc. Thinly spread a few tablespoons of the buttercream over the surface. Pull in the cling film over it.

12 Completely chill the cake for a minimum of 2 hours or up to 24 hours in advance.

13 Once the cake has completely chilled, remove from the fridge, ease it out of the tin and take off the cling film. Place it on a suitable cake plate or cake board, then follow the instructions on page 34 for coating the cake using a cake turntable and a bench scraper.

14 Decorate the cake with fresh or dried edible flowers. Place it in the fridge to chill further for a few hours.

Saffron, mango and cardamom cake

I only make this cake in summer, when Alphonso or Kesar mangoes are in season. You can find canned Alphonso or Kesar mango purée in Asian stores but I find that it lacks the flavour of fresh mangoes. When in season, you can get the right mangoes from specialist food sellers online. Saffron and cardamom are paired with mango in many Indian desserts so I have borrowed flavours from my heritage here.

1 Make the cake following the method on pages 40–1, adding the cardamom with the flour and the saffron with the eggs.

2 While the cake is in the oven, make the mango purée. Put the mango flesh, lime zest and juice, sugar and salt in a pan and cook over a medium heat for 5–6 minutes. Add the cornflour paste and cook for a further 2–3 minutes. Remove from the heat and pass it through a sieve (strainer) to exclude any fibrous strands from the purée. Set aside to cool completely.

3 To make the mango buttercream, whisk all the ingredients together until well combined. Divide into 2 bowls: one for filling, one for coating.

Assembly

4 Wash and dry a 20cm (8in) round cake tin or use a springform cake tin. Line it with 2 layers of cling film (plastic wrap), allowing a ¾in (2cm) overhang.

5 Place one cake disc in the base of the tin. Generously brush it with the saffron-infused milk. Add 5 tablespoons of the mango buttercream and level using the back of a spoon. Add 2–3 tablespoons chopped mango, spreading it over the buttercream but leaving a 2.5cm (1 in) gap around the rim.

6 Place the second cake layer in the tin and repeat with the saffron milk, buttercream and chopped mangoes, as above.

Continued...

- 1 batch Genoise batter (pages 40–1)
- 3–4 green cardamom pods, husks removed, seeds finely powdered
- 10–12 saffron strands crushed to a fine powder, infused in 1 Tbsp water

For the mango purée

- flesh from 4 fresh mangoes – only use Alphonso or Kesar in season
- zest and juice of 1 lime
- 35g (scant ¼ cup) caster (superfine) sugar
- ½ tsp salt
- 1 tsp cornflour (cornstarch) mixed with 1 Tbsp water

For the mango buttercream

- 1 batch of Swiss Meringue Buttercream (pages 52–3)
- 75g (2¾oz) mango purée (see above)
- ¼ tsp ground turmeric

For the filling

- 10 saffron strands infused in 100ml (7 Tbsp) milk
- flesh from 3 ripe mangoes, chopped – only use Alphonso or Kesar

To decorate (optional)

- edible flowers

7 Top with the third cake disc. Generously soak it with the saffron milk. Spread a few tablespoons of the buttercream across the top layer. Pull in the cling film over it.

8 Completely chill the cake for a minimum of 2 hours, or up to 24 hours in advance.

9 Once the cake has completely chilled, remove from the fridge, ease it out of the tin and take off the cling film. Place it on a suitable cake plate or cake board, then follow the instructions on page 34 for coating the cake using a cake turntable and a bench scraper.

10 Decorate the cake with fresh or dried edible flowers. Place it in the fridge to chill further for a few hours.

Index

Acknowledgements

Amit, because of you, I am. You always know how to bring a smile to my face. Thank you for always keeping us safe and together through every hurdle life throws at us. Your unconditional love and presence, you holding my hand through life, is a blessing I am grateful for every day. You by my side to eternity and beyond, and me coming back to a magically clean kitchen after the mess I create, is all I ever want. Also, look where those four words, 'My little cake tin', you scribbled on our 10th anniversary card more than a decade ago led us to....

Thank you Ma and Papa for believing in me and my dreams, always encouraging and nurturing me every step of the way. Papa, your teachings are my very foundations. I have inherited my love for food from you. You taught me everything I know. You also have a sixth sense for me and, like many things, you saw this book coming long before it even came to my mind. Ma, you are my strength and my weakness, you taught me never to give up. I hope I did you both proud.

To my siblings, thank you for eating all the burnt and undercooked cakes through our childhood. Those days led me here. I am thankful every day to have you three in my life. Chinkri, my little sister, thank you for always being there by my side. I cannot do life without you.

Jan and Stu, the edible flower magicians, you have been a constant support through the Mylittlecaketin journey. Organically growing and hand picking each flower to adorn my cakes and helping me grow this dream. Thank you for your words of encouragement and your sweet messages, always. Thank you for growing each and every flower in this book in your new garden just for me. I could not have done it without you. I am eternally grateful to you both.

Thank you, dear Thane Prince, for always guiding me. I cannot thank you enough for all that you have done for me. I want the world to know that this book would not have happened without your kindness and encouragement.

Esther, Vidushi and Toshal, for your friendship and warmth. From ordering the very first cakes and nudging me when I was not sure – and encouraging me all these years ever since.

Martine, my dear agent, thank you for listening to me, putting sense into everything I say and always having my back. You held my hand through it and, at times, believed in this book more than I did.

Food connected us all, but our friendship keeps us together. I am so happy we met and now you all are in for life. Thank you, Sabrina Ghayour, for being a friend with a heart of gold. There is no one like you. Ravneet Gill, for being the pure joy and sunshine that you are. I have only love for you, always. Georgina Hayden, for the words of encouragement and always pushing me forward, and for the love you keep showering me with. Holly O'Neill, my friend, for opening the door for me and letting the light in. Thank you.

A big thank you to the team at Quadrille: Sarah Lavelle, for believing in this project and giving me this opportunity. Thank you for guiding me and making the 'Mylittlecaketin' concept a reality. Sofie Shearman, for editing this book and making sense of my scribbles. Your kind and thoughtful suggestions and edits make this book what it is. I am so happy you understood me. Emily Lapworth, for putting it all together, designing the cover and the book, for your creative direction and the beauty in the pages. You are amazing, and you brought a sense of calm and clarity for me through the process.

Thank you, Kim Lightbody – it was a joy to work with you and an honour to have you photograph this book. Thank you for your attention to detail and for capturing the moments so beautifully.

Katie Marshall – I absolutely think that the photo shoots would not have been so much fun without your hard work and your forward planning. Thank you for baking my recipes with so much enthusiasm, positivity and so many smiles. I could not have done it without you.

Thank you Maria, Lucy and Jess, for your invaluable support on the shoot days in the kitchen.

Faye – thank you for your wonderful selection of props – they helped bring everything together and weave the story.

To all the people who follow me on social media and my friends, family and neighbours – you have all been amazing. I cannot thank you enough for your support. It helped me build up my confidence every step of the way.

Managing Director Sarah Lavelle
Project Editor Sofie Shearman
Design Manager Katherine Case
Art Director & Designer Emily Lapworth
Food Stylist Katie Marshall
Photographer Kim Lightbody
Prop Stylist Faye Wears
Head of Production Stephen Lang
Production Controller Gary Hayes

Disclaimer:
Flowers and plants are consumed at the
reader's own risk. The author and publisher
cannot be held responsible for adverse
reactions or consequences resulting from the
use or misue of information in this book with
regards to the identification, preparation,
handling, consumption and/or storage of
flowers and plants. The reader should consult
a healthcare professional for advice relating
to specific flowers and plants and pre-existing
health conditions, medications, pregnancy,
breastfeeding, allergies or sensitivities.

Published in 2024 by Quadrille,
an imprint of Hardie Grant Publishing

Quadrille
52–54 Southwark Street
London SE1 1UN
quadrille.com

Cataloguing in Publication Data: a catalogue record
for this book is available from The British Library.

Text © Tarunima Sinha 2024
Photography © Kim Lightbody 2024
Illustrations © Madiwaso Art & Galerie Design Studio
via Creative Market 2024
Design © Quadrille 2024

ISBN 978 1 83783 082 4

Printed in China

FSC
www.fsc.org

MIX
Paper | Supporting
responsible forestry
FSC™ C020056